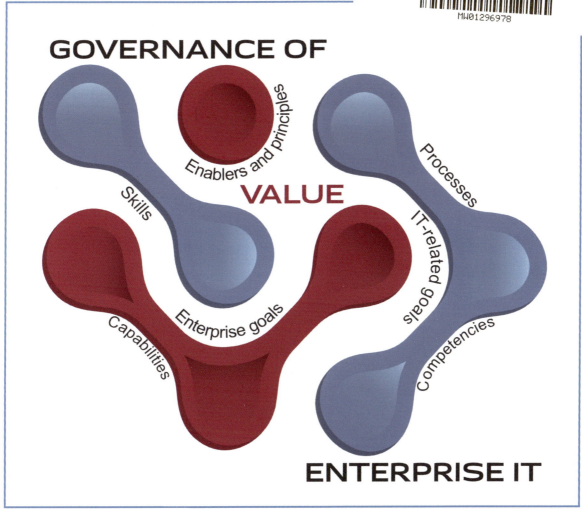

COBIT 5 Foundation Reference and Study Guide

COPYRIGHT NOTICE

This material is licensed solely to a registered learner of The Lean IT Group, LLC. No part of this material may be reproduced, modified, republished, posted, leased, licensed or transferred in any form without prior written consent of The Lean IT Group, LLC.

This material contains proprietary information that is protected by copyright. No part of this material may be photocopied, reproduced, or translated to another language without the prior consent of The Lean IT Group, LLC.

Copyright © The Lean IT Group, LLC unless otherwise stated.

Material in this document has been sourced from the following COBIT® publications:
- COBIT 5 - A Business Framework for the Governance and Management of Enterprise IT
- COBIT - Process Assessment Model (PAM): Using COBIT 5
- COBIT 5 - Enabling Processes
- COBIT 5 - Toolkit

This material has been reproduced under permission of ISACA. All rights reserved.

COBIT® is a trade mark of ISACA®, registered in the United States and other countries, used under permission of ISACA®. All rights reserved.

The sample examination papers included in this publication is a copyright© of ISACA. All rights reserved.

About the Author

Ana Cecilia Delgado is president of The Lean IT Group, a consultancy and software development firm that specializes in business and IT alignment. The Lean IT Group started in Florida, USA and has customers around the world.

Delgado has over 30 years experience in management and technology consulting with extensive hands-on experience in information technology strategy and process improvement. She is certified as a COBIT® Trainer. She has developed official courseware around IT best practices. She was instrumental in the design of LeanCS®, a service management solution developed by The Lean IT Group and certified to ensure that it meets the functional requirements for ITIL® compatibility.

Delgado is a thought leader and has been a speaker at many international conferences on the subject of IT Governance & Business Service Management. She also holds the following recognized certifications: ISO/IEC 20000 Consultant Manager, Business Process Professional, ITIL® Expert, Lean IT Foundation, Microsoft Certified System Engineer, Microsoft Certified Trainer and Cloud Computing among others.

Do you wish to contact the author?
Ana Cecilia Delgado can be reached at simplisaidjournal@gmail.com.com. Her blog http://simplisaid.com also contains useful information on best practices.

Preface

Control Objectives for Information and Related Technology (COBIT) is a framework created by ISACA for information technology (IT) management and IT governance. It is a supporting toolset that allows managers to bridge the gap between control requirements, technical issues and business risks.

The COBIT 5 framework for the governance and management of enterprise IT is a leading-edge business optimization and growth roadmap that leverages proven practices, global thought leadership and ground-breaking tools to inspire IT innovation and fuel business success.

This publication is directed to readers that are interested in understanding the key terms, principles and facts of COBIT 5 at a foundation level and to those learners interested in achieving the COBIT 5 Foundation certification. To ease self-study, the publication has images and tables that contains important and relevant information so please do not pass them over when preparing for the real exam. *A picture says more than many words and 90% of the information that the brain process is visual.*

Associated exam voucher can be purchased at htttps://sophosit.com/store.

Quality training and certification program significantly contributes to the success of any IT initiative. This publication is based on a proven instructor-led accredited course but adapted for self-study at a fraction of time and cost.

Content at a Glance

Chapter 1 - Introduction to COBIT 5 — 3

Chapter 2 - The principles of COBIT 5 — 5

Chapter 3 - The enablers of COBIT 5 — 15

Chapter 4 - Process Reference Model — 27

Chapter 5 - Process Capability Model — 29

Chapter 6 - Implementing COBIT 5 — 33

Appendix A - COBIT 5 Enterprise Goals — 37

Appendix B - Mapping Enterpise Goals to IT Goals — 38

Appendix C - Mapping IT-related Goals to COBIT Processes — 39

Appendix D - Governance and Management Interactions — 42

Appendix E - Organizational Structures Matrix — 43

Appendix F - Information Quality Categories — 45

Appendix G - Skill Categories — 46

Appendix H - Process Reference Model — 47

Appendix I - Process Capability Model — 48

Appendix J - Feetwalk Case Study — 49

Appendix K - Answerkey to Practices — 55

Appendix L - Sample Exam Paper — 59

Appendix M - Answerkey for Sample Exam Paper — 79

Index — 81

Chapter 1 - Introduction to COBIT 5

Information is one of the most critical assets in any enterprise. Information is a key element for business decisions. Information flows across the enterprise's technology infrastructure. Therefore, Information technology (IT) units play an important role in making it available to the business while ensuring it is also trustworthy and confidential. Any investment made in IT must ensure that information generates value to the business, and that all IT-enabled processes contribute to the enterprise's operational excellence. IT resources must be continuously optimized ensuring that associated risks and costs are managed efficiently and effectively and that they're implemented in compliance with legal and regulatory requirements. These challenges can only be overcome with good governance.

Every enterprise, regardless its size and industry, must have governance. *Governance* is the system by which organizations are directed and controlled ensuring that their goals will be achieved. To support the enterprise governance, there should be processes in place that ensure the effective and efficient use of IT in enabling an organization to achieve its goals. This is known as *IT Governance*. COBIT 5 is a comprehensive framework that assists enterprises to achieve their goals and deliver value through effective governance and management of enterprise IT. Good governance requires that the business side and IT units are "rowing in the same direction". For this, the enterprise's senior management must embrace IT as a significant part of the business.

> *Corporate governance* is the system by which organizations are directed and controlled ensuring that their goals will be achieved.
>
> *IT governance* deals with processes required to ensure the effective and efficient use of IT in enabling an organization to achieve its goals.
>
> **COBIT 5** is a comprehensive framework that assists enterprises to achieve their goals and deliver value through effective governance and management of enterprise IT.

COBIT 5 delivers many benefits. Among a long list of benefits, I would like to mention:
- Engages stakeholders.
- Business understands the role of IT.
- Provides guidelines to increase the levels of efficiency, speed and quality of IT-enabled processes.
- Covers the full end-to-end business and IT functional responsibilities.
- IT-enabled investments are driven by value creation.
- Complements with major frameworks such as ITIL®, PMBOK®, PRINCE2®, COSO.

The 5 principles of COBIT 5

COBIT 5 is built around five key principles for an effective governance and management framework. The five principles are intended to develop a good governance and management framework to optimize information and technology investment and use for the benefit of stakeholders. The five principles are:

1. Meeting stakeholders needs.
2. Covering the enterprise end-to-end.
3. Applying a single integrated framework.
4. Enabling a holistic approach.
5. Separating governance from management.

Figure 1 illustrates the COBIT 5 Principles:

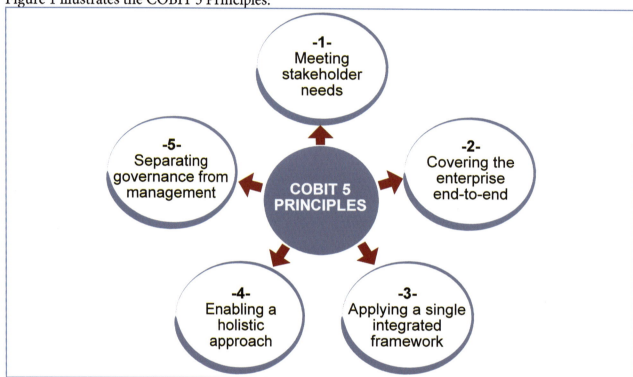

FIGURE 1 - Reproduced under permission of ISACA. All rights reserved.

Having a good understanding of these principles is essential to build an effective governance and management framework. In Chapter 2, I will cover each principle in-depth.

Chapter 2 - The principles of COBIT 5

Principle 1 - Meeting stakeholders needs

One key characteristic of effective governance and management framework is value creation. Value can only be created if we understand the stakeholders' needs. This can be accomplish by asking three key questions:
- Who will receive the benefits?
- Who will take over the associated risks?
- What resources are needed?

> *Value creation* is about realizing benefits at an optimal resource cost while optimizing risk.

Why these questions? Because value creation is about realizing benefits at an optimal resource cost while optimizing risk. Therefore, the following objectives must be achieved to create value which in turn, represents the governance objective:
- *Benefits realization* - delivering IT services and solutions that fit-for-purpose, on time and within budget, and generating the financial and non-financial benefits that were intended.
- *Risk optimization* - preserving value by addressing the business risk associated with the use, ownership, operation, involvement, influence and adoption of IT within an enterprise.
- *Resource optimization* - ensuring that the appropriate capabilities are in place to execute the strategic plan and sufficient, appropriate and effective resources are provided.

Figure 2 illustrates how to achieve value creation:

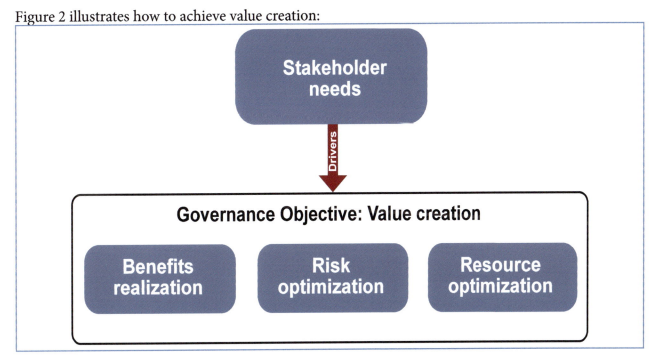

FIGURE 2 - Reproduced under permission of ISACA. All rights reserved.

Enterprises have different meanings and views of 'value' so this must be well-understood before trying to create value. Governance is about negotiating and deciding amongst different stakeholders' value interests. By consequence, the governance system should consider all stakeholders when making benefit, risk and resource assessment decisions.

Stakeholders' needs are influenced by internal and external factors such as changes in business strategy, new regulations, new technologies, etc. Stakeholders' needs must be translated into specific actions leading to the achievement of the enterprise's goals. The *goals cascade* in COBIT 5 is the recommended mechanism to translate these needs into an actionable strategy.

> The *goals cascade* is a top-down approach use to map stakeholders' needs to specific goals to support the enterprise's needs with the most adequate IT solutions and services.

How the goals cascade works?
The goals cascade helps to prioritize IT initiatives based on business changing needs and strategic objectives. It translates stakeholders' needs into relevant and tangible goals and identifies which enablers are the most important to achieve enterprise goals. The enablers identify which specific aspects of COBIT 5 can be used as a guidance for the implementation of identified improvements initiatives. These enablers are categorized as P for 'primary' and S for 'secondary'. Primary means there is an important relationship or represents a primary support for goal achievement. Secondary is used when the relationship or support level is strong but less important.

Figure 3 illustrates an overview of the goals cascade:

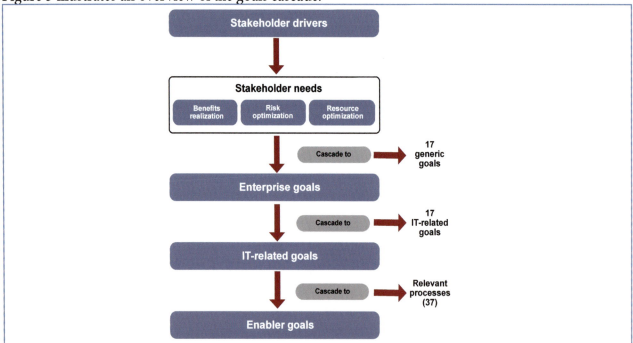

FIGURE 3 - Reproduced under permission of ISACA. All rights reserved.

The goals cascade involves four steps:
1. Understanding the drivers that serves as a stimulus for change.
2. Relating stakeholder needs to enterprise goals.
3. Mapping enterprise goals to IT-related goals.
4. Applying enablers to a set of specific and relevant IT-related goals.

As a guideline, COBIT 5 provides a set of generic enterprise goals that can be used to map the identified stakeholders' needs. These enterprise goals are grouped using the four dimensions of the balanced scorecard (BSC[1]) represented by a list of commonly used goals that an enterprise may define for itself. Bear in mind that this list is not written "in stone" and does not include all possible enterprise goals. However, most of the stakeholders' needs can be easily mapped onto one or more of the generic enterprise goals included in COBIT 5. APPENDIX A contains a table of the 17 generic enterprise goals.

Achieving enterprise goals requires IT to produce specific outcomes within the context of COBIT 5 which only considers IT-related activities and goals. Therefore, the enterprise goals must be mapped to specific IT-related goals. COBIT 5 provides a set of generic IT-related goals that can be used to map them to the enterprise goals identified in step 2. APPENDIX B contains a matrix mapping each enterprise goal to primary and secondary IT-related goals. The best way to understand the goals cascade and its relationship is by applying the concept in a real-world scenario. For this purpose, I have included a case study of a fictional enterprise that goes from being an online retailer to a service provider: **Feetwalk**. Feetwalk faces challenges similar of any enterprise that is forced to change its enterprise goals due to internal and external factors such as a downturn economy. Let's apply the concepts of the goals cascade to this scenario:

Practice - The goals cascade
The business strategy at Feetwalk is about to change. A decision was made to generate more revenue by sharing the IT infrastructure with manufacturing companies. Read APPENDIX J and complete the following activities:
1. Refer to Appendix A and identify 3 key enterprise goals that are considered priorities to ensure the success of "Powered by Feetwalk".
2. Map the identified enterprise goals in step 1 to primary IT-related goals using Appendix B.

NOTE: When applying the goals cascade, consider:
- The enterprise's corporate culture, its priorities, goals and objectives.
- How a change in business strategy impact behaviors.
- The enterprise's specific environment, size, industry, etc.

---

[1] BSC is a management system for improving organizational performance in four key dimensions. It is based on the premise that "what you measure is what you get".

Answer key is provided in APPENDIX K. Bear in mind that you may have selected different enterprise goals and this is fine. What is really important is that the enterprise goals are correctly mapped to the IT-related goals.

Principle 2 - Covering the enterprise end-to-end

There should be a seamless integration of IT governance with the enterprise governance. COBIT 5 allows this integration by providing a holistic view of both forms of governance. COBIT 5 considers all functions and processes required to govern and manage enterprise information and related technologies.

The end-to-end approach consists of 4 key elements as illustrated in Figure 4:

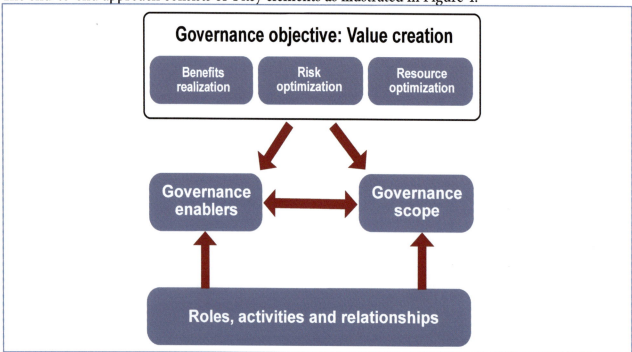

FIGURE 4 - Reproduced under permission of ISACA. All rights reserved.

1. *Value creation* - realizing benefits at an optimal resource cost while optimizing risk.
2. *Governance enablers* - the organizational resources for governance, such as frameworks, principles, structures, processes, practices people and information. Enablers also include resources such as the IT infrastructure and applications that produce service capabilities.
3. *Governance scope* - how much of the organization are we interested in? Will governance apply to the entire organization or to a specific legal entity or asset? If there are different views of governance, a different scope can be applied to each view.
4. *Roles, activities and relationships* - determine who is involved in governance, what they do within the governance system and how they interact. Roles, responsibilities and activities are differentiated between those related to governance which belongs to the governing body and those related to management which belong to management and operations.

Governing body sets direction and monitors the performance and compliance of agreed-on direction.

Management is responsible for monitoring that direction set by the governance body is being applied.

Figure 5 illustrates the roles, activities and relationships:

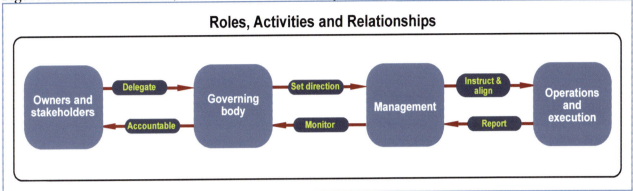

FIGURE 5 - Reproduced under permission of ISACA. All rights reserved.

Principle 3 - Applying a single integrated framework

COBIT 5 is a single integrated framework. It is aligned to other latest relevant standards and frameworks allowing its effective integration. It provides:

- A guidance written in a non-technical, technology-agnostic common language.
- A simple architecture with guidelines to produce consistent solutions.
- A seamless integration with different ISACA frameworks.

Figure 6 illustrates the components of COBIT 5 to build a single integrated governance framework:

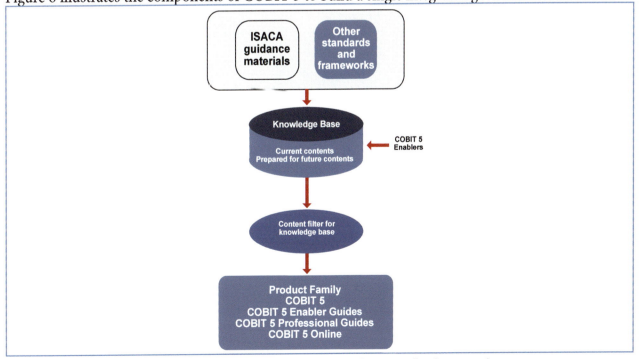

FIGURE 6 - Reproduced under permission of ISACA. All rights reserved.

COBIT 5 is considered the most comprehensive and updated business framework for governance and management of enterprise IT.

ISACA continually researches for new trends and develop new content tempered to current factors that affect governance and management of IT while ensuring its compatibility and integration with existing ISACA guidance such as COBIT 4.1, Val IT 2.0, Risk IT, etc. COBIT 5 is also aligned to other relevant standards and frameworks, such as ITIL, TOGAF and ISO standards.

The knowledge base contains all guidance and content produced now and its structure is ready for future content providing a sound and comprehensive reference base of good practices.

Principle 4 - Enabling a holistic approach

Enablers are individual or collective factors that influence whether something will work. A governance enabler will directly influence the outcome of enterprise governance. Enablers are driven by the goals cascade defining what the different enablers should achieve. Frameworks, principles, processes, practices and structures are examples of enablers.

Figure 7 illustrates the seven categories of enabler in COBIT 5:

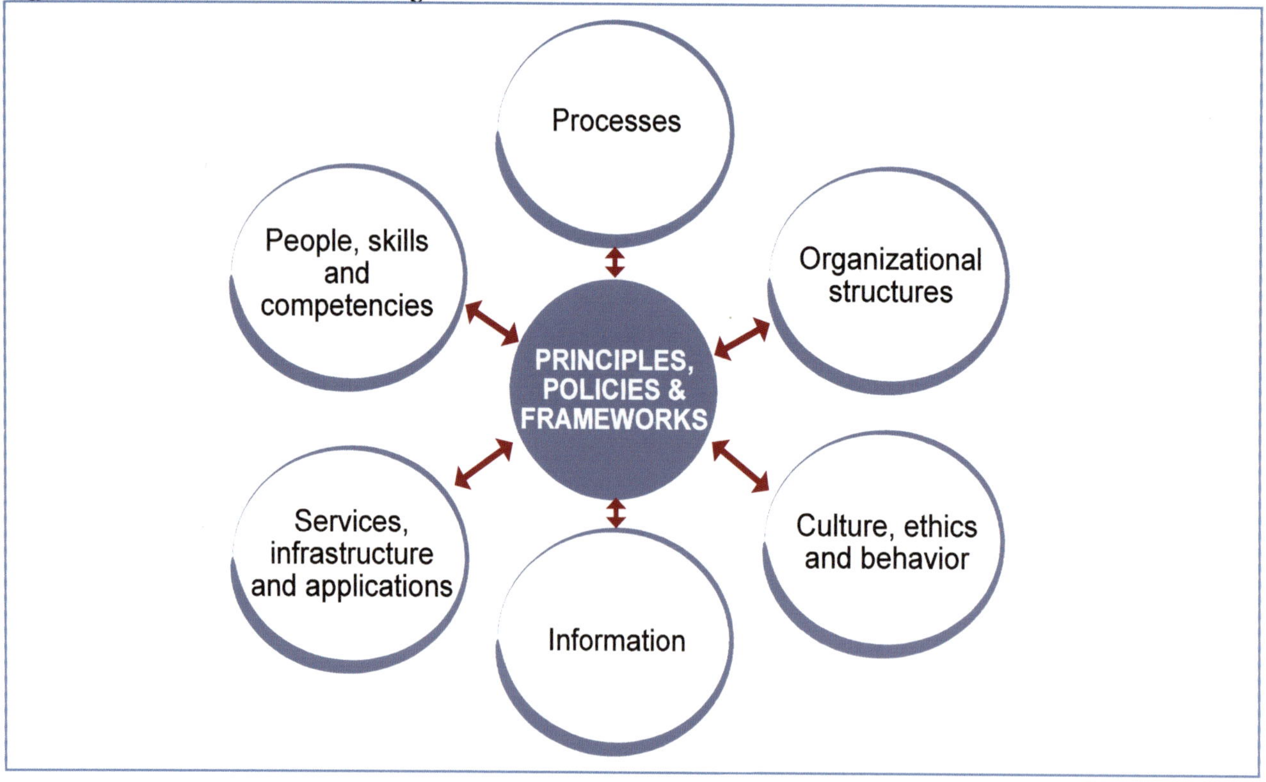

FIGURE 7 - Reproduced under permission of ISACA. All rights reserved.

As you can see in the illustration, enablers are interconnected. An enabler needs input from the other enablers to be effective. Each enabler delivers benefits to other enablers by producing outputs.

In Chapter 3, enablers will be covered in-depth but first, let me provide a brief description of each category:
1. *Principles, policies and frameworks* - the vehicle to translate the desired behavior into practical guidance for day-to-day management.
2. *Processes* - a set of practices and activities to achieve certain objectives and produce a set of outputs in support of achieving overall IT-related goals.
3. *Organizational structures* - the key decision-making entities in an enterprise.
4. *Culture, ethics and behavior* - the behavior of individuals and of the enterprise which are normally underestimated as a success factor in governance and management activities.
5. *Information* - all information produced and used by the enterprise. Information is required for keeping the organization running and well governed, but at the operational level, information is very often the key product of the enterprise itself and is considered a service capability.
6. *Services, infrastructure and applications* - the infrastructure, technology and applications that provide the enterprise with information technology processing and services.
7. *People, skills and competencies* - required for successful completion of all activities and for making correct decisions and taking corrective actions.

> *These enablers are also enterprise resources:*
> - Information
> - Services, infrastructure and applications
> - People, skills and competencies

To provide a holistic view, enablers must have:
- *Stakeholders* - the parties who play an active role and/or have an interest in the enabler.
- *Goals* - state the expected outcomes of the enabler and how it will apply and operate.
- *Lifecycle* - the cycle from inception through an operational/useful life until disposal.
- *Good practices* - support the achievement of the enabler goals.

Principle 5 - Separating governance from management

The COBIT 5 framework makes a clear distinction between governance and management. These two disciplines encompass different types of activities, require different organizational structures and serve different purposes.

Governance is about ensuring that stakeholder needs, conditions and options are evaluated to determine balanced, agreed-on enterprise objectives to be achieved; setting direction through prioritization and decision making; and monitoring performance and compliance against agreed-on direction and objectives.

Management is about planning, building, running and monitoring (PBRM) activities in alignment with the direction set by the governance body to achieve the enterprise objectives.

The COBIT 5 process reference model divides the governance and management processes of enterprise IT into two main process categories:

- *Governance processes* which deal with the stakeholder governance objectives—value delivery, risk optimization and resource optimization—and include practices and activities aimed at evaluating strategic options, providing direction to IT and monitoring the outcome. The governance processes are five and they are grouped under Evaluate, Direct and Monitor (EDM) domain in the process reference model. APPENDIX H contains a detailed matrix of all processes in COBIT 5.
- *Management processes* which refers to the practices and activities in management processes covering the responsibility areas of PBRM (plan, build, run and monitor) enterprise IT, and they have to provide end-to-end coverage of IT. Management processes are grouped in four domains: Align, Plan and Organize (APO); Build, Acquire and Implement (BAI); Deliver, Service and Support (DSS) and Monitor, Evaluate and Assess (MEA).

COBIT 5 is not prescriptive, but it advocates that enterprises implement governance and management processes such that the key areas are covered, as shown in Figure 8:

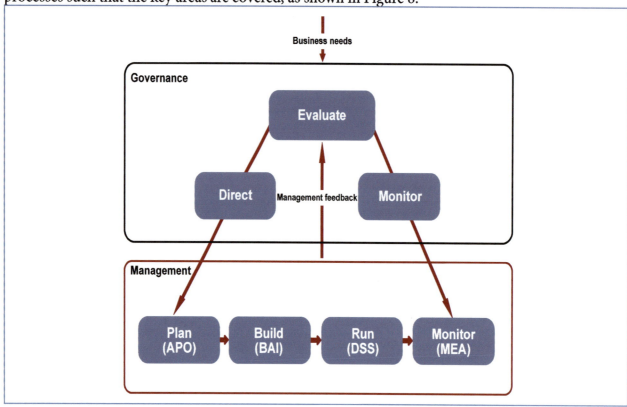

FIGURE 8 - Reproduced under permission of ISACA. All rights reserved.

An enterprise can organize its processes as they fit, as long as all necessary governance and management objectives are covered. Smaller enterprises may have fewer processes; larger and more complex enterprises may have many processes, all to cover the same objectives.

Governance and management have different types of activities and different responsibilities. However, a set of interactions is required between governance and management to build and sustain an efficient and effective governance system.

These interactions, using the enabler structure, are shown at a high level in APPENDIX D.

Chapter 3 - The enablers of COBIT 5

As mentioned in Chapter 2, enabler is defined as:

> An individual or collective factor that influence whether something will work. Enablers are driven by the goals cascade defining what the different enablers should achieve.

Enablers are interconnected. An enabler needs input from the other enablers to be effective. Each enabler produce outputs to other enablers which in turn, are translated into benefits.

Enabler dimensions

To deal with the stakeholders' needs, all interrelated enablers have to be analyzed for relevance and addressed if required. To facilitate this analysis, COBIT 5 defines four common dimensions that each enabler must have. This are known as the *enabler dimensions*, a simplified and structured way to deal with enablers.

Figure 9 illustrates a graphical view of the enabler dimensions:

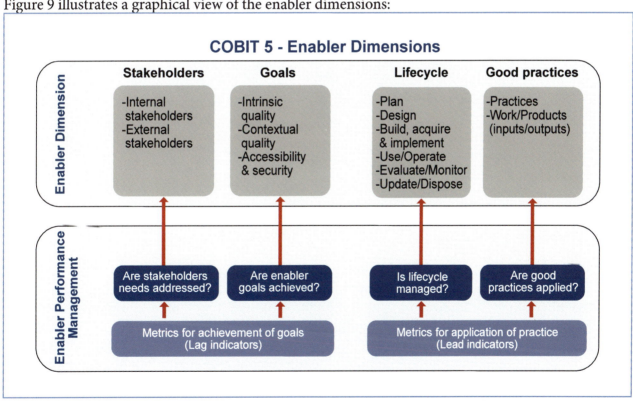

FIGURE 9 - Reproduced under permission of ISACA. All rights reserved.

Stakeholders

Each enabler has stakeholders, the parties who play an active role and/or have an interest in the enabler. The can be internal or external. Stakeholders have their own interests and needs and these needs must be translated to enterprise goals.

Goals

Each enabler has goals that lead to benefits realization if they are achieved. They define the enabler's outcomes and/or its reason for being. Goals are categorized as of:

- *Intrinsic quality* - goals work accurately, are objectives and provide accurate, objetive and reputable results.
- *Contextual quality* - their outcomes are fit for the purpose. Outcomes should be relevant, complete, current, appropriate, consistent, understandable and easy to use.
- *Access & security* - enablers are available as needed and outcomes are secured ensuring restricted access to those entitled to.

Lifecycle

Each enabler has a life cycle, from inception through an operational/useful life until disposal. The lifecycle phases of enablers are:
1. Plan
2. Design
3. Build, acquire and implement
4. Use/Operate
5. Evaluate/Monitor
6. Update/Dispose

Good practices

Good practices should be defined for each enabler. They support the achievement of the enabler goals and provide guidance on how best to implement the enabler. Good practices help to define the required inputs and outputs for each enabler. Other standards and frameworks can be used.

Enabler performance management

Enterprises expect positive outcomes from the application and use of enablers. To monitor performance on a regular basis, key performance indicators and related metrics must be defined. When defining performance indicators, establish a balance between *lag* indicators and *lead* indicators.

Lag indicators are output-oriented. They are aimed to measure if enabler's outcome is achieved. When reporting results, this is what the business is interested in. Questions should be answered by lag indicators:
- Are stakeholder needs addressed?
- Are enabler goals achieved?

Lead indicators are input-oriented. They are aimed to measure enabler's performance and they represent what the IT provider must monitor continuously. Questions should be answered by lead indicators:
- Is the enabler life cycle managed?
- Are good practices applied?

Chapter 3 - The enablers of COBIT 5

Detailed description of COBIT 5 enablers

Principles, policies and frameworks

Principles and policies refer to the communication mechanisms put in place to convey the governing body's and management's direction and instructions. The are applied to communicate the rules of the enterprise, in support of the governance objectives and enterprise values.

Key terms

Principle - a proposition that serves as the foundation for good behavior.
Policy - a detailed guidance on how to put principles into practice.
Framework - the set of ideas, information, and principles that form the structure of an organization.

Stakeholders

Stakeholders can be internal or external. They are grouped in:
- The stakeholders that define a set of policies.
- The stakeholders that align and comply with the policies set.

Goals and metrics

The goals and metrics defined for each principle must:
- Be limited in number and expressed in simple language.
- Each principle must contain policies that are:
  - Effective - aimed to achieve the stated purpose.
  - Efficient - ensuring that principles are implemented in the most efficient way.
  - Non-intrusive - do not create unnecessary resistance.
  - Accessible - available to stakeholders as needed.

Good practices - as shown in Figure 10

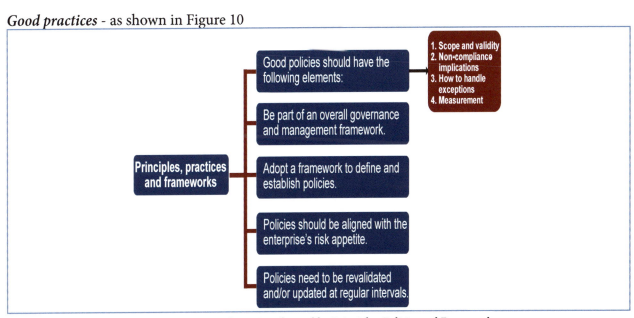

FIGURE 10 - Good practices for enabler Principles, Policies and Framework

Relationships - as shown in Figure 11

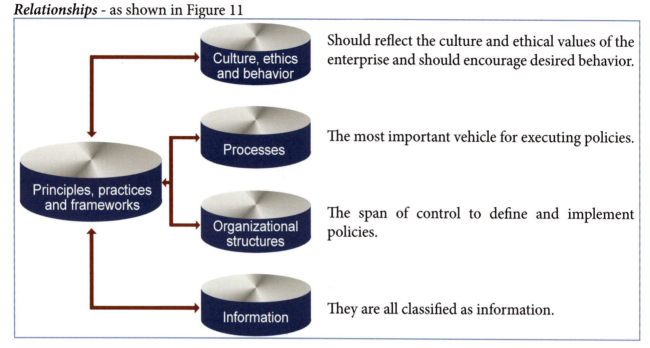

FIGURE 11 - Relationships for enabler Principles, Policies and Framework

Processes

A process is defined as *"a collection of practices influenced by the enterprise's policies and procedures that takes inputs from a number of sources (including other processes), manipulates the inputs and produces outputs".*

Stakeholders

Stakeholders are grouped in:
- External stakeholders which include customers, business partners, shareholders and regulators.
- Internal stakeholders which include the board, management, staff and volunteers.

Goals and metrics

A *process goal* is a statement describing the desired outcome of a process. Process goals support IT-related goals. An *outcome* can be an artifact, a significant change of a state or a significant improvement to process capability. Goals can be:
- *Intrinsic* - aimed to ensure that the process is accurate, complies with rules and is in line with good practice.
- *Contextual* - aimed to ensure that the process is adequate, relevant, well-understood and easy to apply.
- *Accessible and secure* - aimed to ensure that the process remains confidential, that only those who need it, will have access.

To manage the enabler effectively and efficiently, metrics need to be defined to measure the extent to which the expected outcomes are achieved. Metrics should be **SMART - Specific, measurable, actionable, relevant and time bound.**

Lifecycle - as shown in Figure 12

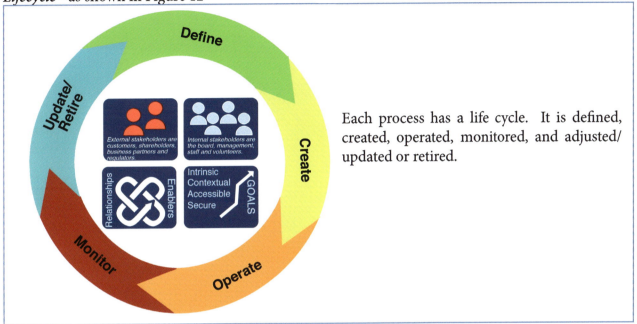

Each process has a life cycle. It is defined, created, operated, monitored, and adjusted/updated or retired.

FIGURE 12 - The lifecycle for the enabler Process

Good practices - as shown in Figure 13

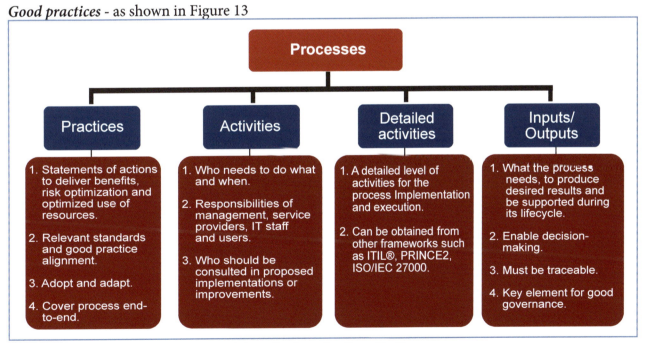

FIGURE 13 - Good practices for enabler Processes

There are other frameworks that provide detailed information on how to apply these practices. You can refer to these sources as a complement to COBIT as long as they are aligned to COBIT 5 Process

Reference Model (APPENDIX H). COBIT 5 Enabling Process is a publication that describes these practices with a great level of detail.

Relationships - as shown in Figure 14

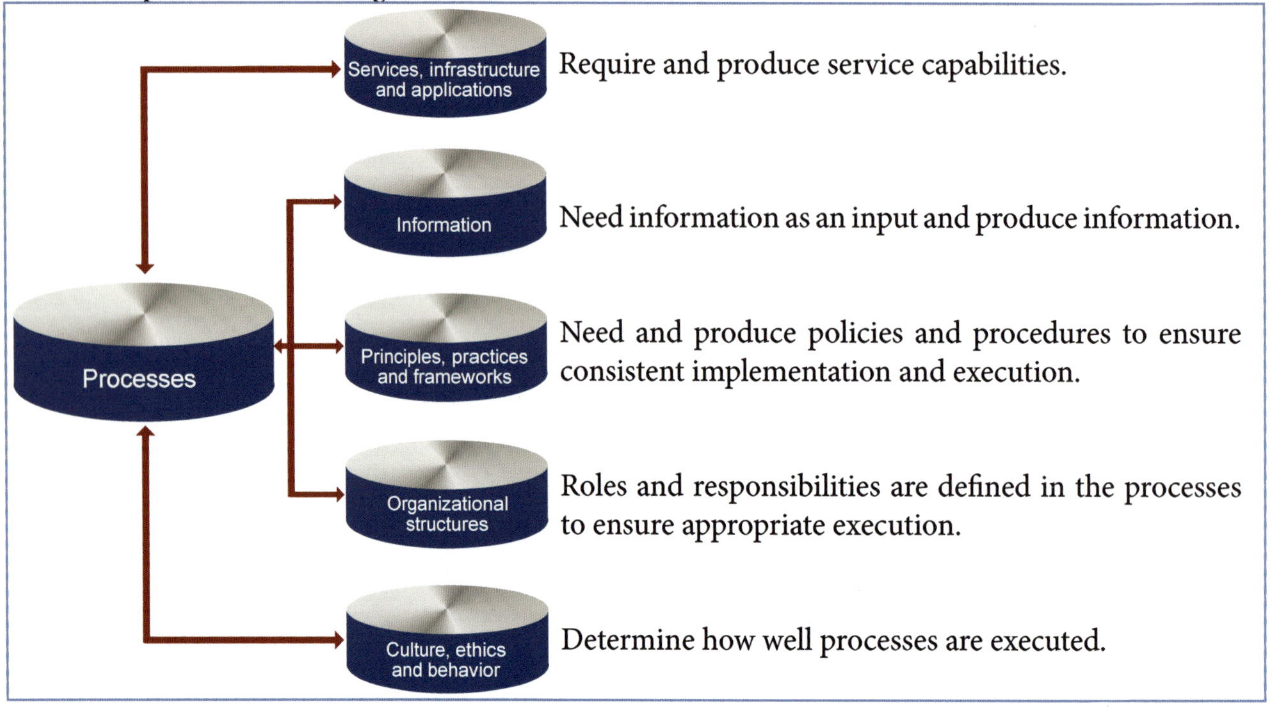

- Services, infrastructure and applications: Require and produce service capabilities.
- Information: Need information as an input and produce information.
- Principles, practices and frameworks: Need and produce policies and procedures to ensure consistent implementation and execution.
- Organizational structures: Roles and responsibilities are defined in the processes to ensure appropriate execution.
- Culture, ethics and behavior: Determine how well processes are executed.

FIGURE 14 - Relationships for enabler Processes

Bear in mind that any process may interface with other processes as they do not operate isolated.

Organizational structures

COBIT 5 proposes 26 roles with a description of their responsibilities. These roles should be used as a guidance. However, these roles and their descriptions remain valid for most of the enterprises. The process model includes RACI charts, which use a number of these roles and structures.

APPENDIX E is a matrix that contains the roles included in COBIT 5 and a brief description of each role.

Stakeholders

Stakeholders can be internal and external to the enterprise, and they include the individual members of the organizational entities, clients, suppliers and regulators.

Goals

Goals for organizational structures must ensure that the operating principles and good practices are efficient and effective in delivering the intended outcomes from the organizational structures and that they enable a good decision-making process.

Lifecycle

An organizational structure has a lifecycle. It is created, exists and is adjusted, and eventually it can be dissolved. A purpose statement and a mandate must be defined during its creation.

Good practices - as shown in Figure 15

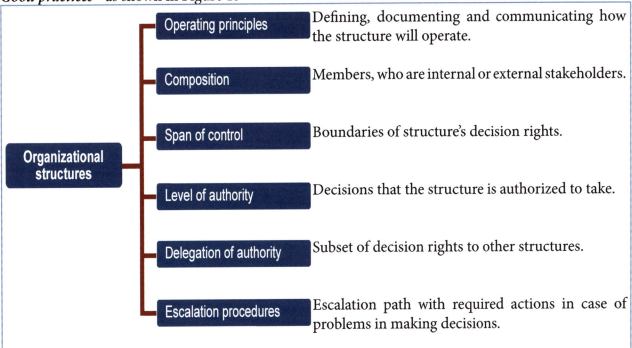

FIGURE 15 - Good practices for enabler Organizational structures

Relationships
- RACI charts link process activities to organizational structures and/or individual roles in the enterprise.
- Culture, ethics and behavior determine the efficiency and effectiveness of organizational structures and their decisions.
- Adequate people, skills and competencies are essential for an efficient and effective organizational structures.
- Organizational structures are guided by the policy framework in place.

Culture, ethics and behavior

Culture, ethics and behavior refers to the set of individual and collective behaviors within an enterprise.

Stakeholders

Stakeholders can be internal or external. There are grouped in:
- The stakeholders responsible for defining, implementing and enforcing desired behaviors.
- The stakeholders that align and comply with the defined rules and norms.

Lifecycle

The lifecycle initiates with an assessment of the existing culture. Assessment's outputs are used as a baseline to identify what changes are required and define a plan to work towards their implementation.

Good practices
- Communication and awareness throughout the enterprise of desired behaviors and the underlying corporate values.
- "Leading by example" from senior management and other champions to motivate desired behavior.
- Incentives to encourage and deterrents to enforce desired behavior.
- Rules and norms, which provide more guidance on desired organizational behavior.

Goals - as shown in Figure 16

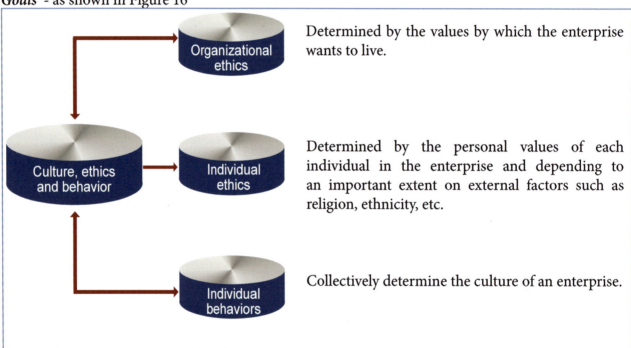

FIGURE 16 - Goals for enabler Culture, ethics and behavior

Relationships

Enabler	Relationship
Processes	It is not enough to design perfect processes but to ensure they are executed as defined to achieve intended outcomes.
Organizational structures	Must be able to make decisions as needed for a decent governance and management of enterprise IT.
Principles, policies and framework	A very important communication mechanism for corporate values and desired behavior.

Information

The enabler deals with <u>all</u> information that is relevant throughout any enterprise including business processes. Business processes generate and process data, transforming them into information and knowledge, and ultimately generating value for the enterprise. The scope of the information enabler mainly concerns the 'information' phase in the information cycle, but the aspects of data and knowledge are also covered in COBIT 5. The information cycle is illustrated in Figure 17:

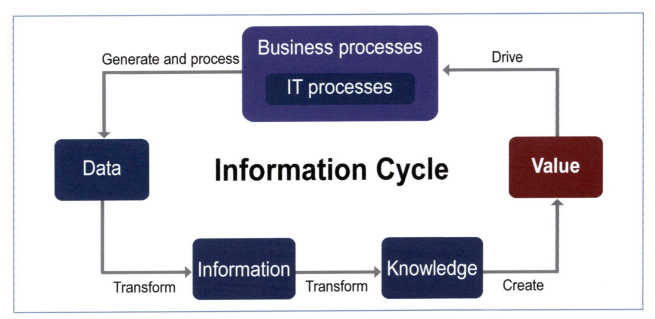

FIGURE17 - Reproduced under permission of ISACA. All rights reserved.

Stakeholders

There are three types of information stakeholders that help to understand their interests and their roles in dealing with information:
- The information producer who is responsible for creating the information.
- The information custodian who is responsible for storing and maintaining the information.
- The information consumer, responsible for using the information.

Goals

Providing quality information is crucial for good governance and management of enterprise IT. COBIT 5 provides seven information quality categories that must be considered to ensure that information is accurate, fit the purpose, accessible and confidential. Refer to APPENDIX F for a complete list.

Information model

COBIT 5 will publish a separate publication with a new and rich information model to make information more tangible and relevant for governance and management of enterprise IT. The information model is intended to mainly address how enterprises should deal with information and how to make it valuable for the enterprise.

This model can be used to:
- Build information system specifications.
- Define requirements for information security.
- Model of application control practices.
- Develop the internal control system.

Services, Infrastructure and Applications

Services can be delivered by internal or external parties—internal IT departments, operations managers, outsourcing providers. Users of services can also be internal— business users—and external to the enterprise—partners, clients, suppliers.

Stakeholders

Services can be delivered by internal or external parties. Business users that use the service are internal stakeholders. There are enterprises that also deliver and support services to external stakeholders such as partners, clients, suppliers.

Service capabilities

Services, infrastructure and applications, in conjunction with processes as shown in Figure 14, are aimed to produce service capabilities and deliver IT-enabled services. Figure 18 illustrates how this enabler can produce these capabilities:

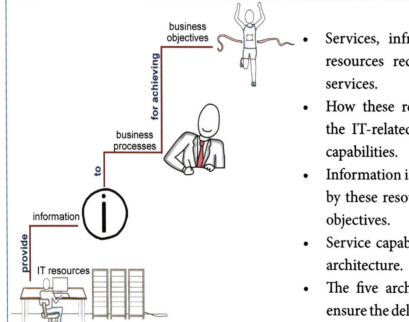

- Services, infrastructure and applications are resources required to deliver the IT-related services.
- How these resources are managed to deliver the IT-related services are considered service capabilities.
- Information is a key service capability produced by these resources and contributes to business objectives.
- Service capabilities are described in a baseline architecture.
- The five architecture principles are aimed to ensure the delivery of quality IT-related services.

Figure 18 - Services, infrastructure and applications

Architecture principles

There are five architecture principles that govern the implementation and use of IT-related resources:
1. *Reuse* - common components of the architecture should be used when designing and implementing solutions.
2. *Buy vs. build* - solutions should be purchased unless there is an approved rationale for developing them.
3. *Simplicity* - the enterprise architecture should be designed and maintained to be as simple as possible.
4. *Agility* - the enterprise architecture should incorporate agility to meet changing business needs.
5. *Openness* - the enterprise architecture should leverage open industry standards.

Relationships - as shown in Figure 19

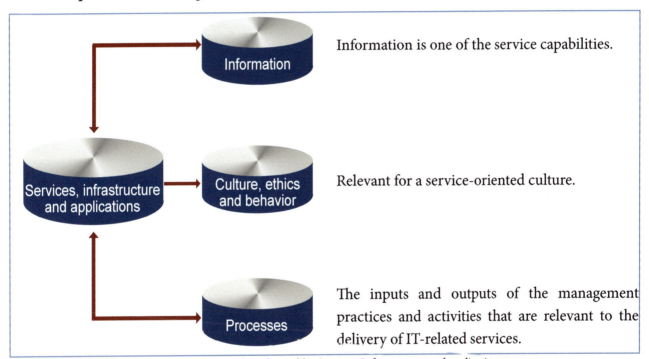

Information is one of the service capabilities.

Relevant for a service-oriented culture.

The inputs and outputs of the management practices and activities that are relevant to the delivery of IT-related services.

Figure 19 - Relationships for enabler Services, Infrastructure and applications

People, skills and competencies

People, skills and competencies are required for the successful completion of all activities and for making correct decisions and taking corrective actions. Therefore, it is of paramount importance to have the adequate people with adequate skills and competencies. To accomplish this task:
1. Define the need for objective skill requirements for each role.
2. Map the different skill categories to COBIT 5 process domains. (Refer to Appendix G).
3. Assess skills at least once a year to plan for the development or acquisition of new skills to fulfill the enterprise changing needs.

Working with enablers

Practice - Mapping IT-related goals to COBIT 5 processes

Processes are key enablers to produce the expected outcomes from the IT-related goals. In practice 1, you have identified the IT-related goals to ensure the success of "Powered by Feetwalk".

Using Appendix C, identify which processes should be implemented to produce the expected outcomes from the IT-related goals identified in the previous practice.

Answer key is provided in APPENDIX K. Bear in mind that you may have selected different IT-related goals and this is fine. What is really important is that the IT-related goals are correctly mapped to the COBIT 5 processes.

Practice - Organizational structures

Using the information from previous practices, the challenges that faces Feetwalk with the new business strategy "Powered by Feetwalk" and Appendix E, identify five (5) roles that you consider are critical for the successful implementation of "Powered by Feetwalk" and its ongoing support. Indicate which person do you think should assume each role based on the information provided in the case study.

Answer key is provided in APPENDIX K.

Chapter 4 - Process Reference Model

In Chapter 2, I briefly introduced the process reference model of COBIT 5 when explaining the principle 5 - *Separating governance from management*. As mentioned, COBIT 5 divides the governance and management processes of enterprise IT into two main areas of responsibility: *governance processes and management processes*.

> The *process reference model* is a comprehensive model that includes governance and management processes normally found in an enterprise relating to IT activities with a clear and detailed description of each process.

Appendix H shows the complete set of 37 governance and management processes within COBIT 5. A detailed description of each process is out of the scope of this publication.

The 37 processes in COBIT 5 are grouped in five domains:

Area of responsibility	Domain	Prefix
Governance	• Evaluate, Direct and Monitor	EDM
Management	• Align, Plan and Organize	APO
	• Build, Acquire and Implement	BAI
	• Deliver, Service and Support	DSS
	• Monitor, Evaluate and Assess	MEA

The processes are placed in the domains in line with the most relevant area of activity considering both working entities, the enterprise and IT.

Each process described in the process reference model has five key components:
1. *Identification* - includes the domain prefix and number, the domain name, the process name and its area of responsibility.
2. *Description* - what the process does and a high-level overview of how it accomplishes its purpose.
3. *Purpose* - description of the overall purpose of the process.
4. *Goals cascade* - the reference and description of the IT-related goals that are primarily supported by the process and the metrics for the IT-related goals.
5. *Goals and metrics* - a set of process goals and a limited number of metrics.

Each process must have defined process practices, how the work is organized. must be well-documented with at least the following elements:
- It is identified with a unique and relevant title.
- It has a description.
- It includes inputs and outputs, with indication of origin and destination.
- It has activities for further detailing the process practice.

The process reference model includes a RACI chart assigning the level of responsibility for process practices to the different roles and structures. The following table describes each level of responsibility:

R	A	C	I
Responsible	Accountable	Consulted	Informed
Who is getting the task done?	Who accounts for the success of the task?	Who is providing input?	Who is receiving information?
Roles taking the main operational stake in fulfilling the activity listed and creating the intended outcome.	Assigns the overall accountability for getting the task done. It cannot be shared.	Roles that provide input to obtain information from other units or external partners.	Roles who are informed of the achievements and/or deliverables of the task.

The process reference model is an excellent reference guide to define processes in your organization. However, this is not prescriptive. You have to adapt them to your enterprise needs considering environmental and culture factors. Also consider additional guidance from other standards and frameworks that complement COBIT.

Chapter 5 - Process Capability Model

The *process capability model* in COBIT 5 is based on the internationally recognized ISO/IEC 15504[2] Software Engineering—Process Assessment standard. This model provides a means to measure the performance of any of the governance (EDM-based) processes or management (PBRM-based) processes, and will allow areas for improvement to be identified.

The process capability model uses the process reference model as guidance to define the requirements for each process capability level. APPENDIX I shows the Process Capability Model with an explanation of the different capability levels and process attributes. It also includes the rating scale used in model.

Process Assessment Model (PAM)

The first step to implement a Governance Enterprise IT (GEIT) program within the organization is to benchmark current processes' capability. The organization needs to perform a health check comparing the "as-is" situation with the "to-be" state benchmarked with a proven and comprehensive governance framework such as COBIT 5.

COBIT 5 provides an evidence-based assessment tool to reliably, consistently and repeatably assess IT process capabilities. Process Assessment Model (PAM) is the only assessment model that provides an enterprise-level view of IT process capability, providing an end-to-end business view of IT's ability to create value. It provides specific actions to measure and monitor current capabilities. From the assessment results, you can produce a gap analysis report to justify improvement initiatives. Based on the process reference model, it also helps business leaders to link enterprise goals to enterprise-related IT goals.

To perform the process capability assessment, based on the process assessment model (PAM), COBIT provides two complementary resources:
- *Self-assessment guide* - a "stand-alone" publication, which can be used by organizations to perform a less rigorous assessment of the capability of their IT processes. This may be a precursor to undertaking more rigorous, evidenced-based assessment.
- *Assessor guide* - intended primarily to support those undertaking process assessments using the formal COBIT PAM. It can be used by team members involved in process assessments to understand what steps need to be taken and how those steps work together. It also can be used by internal auditors to enhance their existing audit scope. It is a valuable reference to the organization's management and stakeholders because it allows them to fully understand the expectations, outcomes and steps in undertaking an assessment.

---

2 ISO/IEC 15504 Information technology – Process assessment, also termed Software Process Improvement and Capability Determination (SPICE), is a set of technical standards documents for the computer software development process and related business management functions.

The capability level of the process consider four key objectives taken from ISO/IEC 15504:
- *Process purpose* - the high-level measurable objectives of performing the process and the likely outcomes of effective implementation of the process.
- *Process outcome* - an observable result of a process.
- *Base practice* - an activity that, when consistently performed, contributes to achieving a specific process purpose.
- *Work product* - an artifact associated with the execution of a process.

The process capability is determined on the achievement of specific process attributes. These specific attributes lead to a capability level of the process being assessed. ISO/IEC 15504 defines six levels of capabilities as illustrated in this table:

Capability level	Definition based on ISO/IEC 15504
Level 0 - Incomplete	The process is not implemented or fails to achieve its purpose.
Level 1 - Performed	The implemented process achieves its process purpose.
Level 2 - Managed	The process is implemented in a managed fashion and its work products are appropriately established, controlled and maintained.
Level 3 - Established	The process, as defined, is capable of achieving its process outcomes.
Level 4 - Predictable	The process is established and operates within defined limits to achieve its process outcomes.
Level 5 - Optimizing	The process is continuously improved to meet relevant current and projected business goals.

> A *process attribute* is a measurable characteristic of process capability applicable to any process.
>
> An *attribute rating* is a judgement of the degree of achievement of the process attribute for the assessed process.

How rating scale works

Reviewing the process outcomes as they are described for each process in the detailed process descriptions, and using the ISO/IEC 15504 rating scale, a rating is assigned to the process being assessed based on the degree each objective is being achieved.

Achieving a particular capability level requires that the process is rated **L** (largely achieved) or **F** (fully achieved). Moving to the next level requires that all attributes of previous level are rated **F** *(fully achieved)*.

Example: If PA 2.1 is **L** (largely achieved) and PA2.2 **F** (fully achieved), the process is in Level 2 even if the attributes of Level 3 are **F**.

This table shows the rating scale with definitions:

Rating scale	Description
N = Not achieved	- There is little or no evidence of achievement of the defined attribute in the assessed process. - 0%-15% achievement.
P = Partially achieved	- There is some evidence of an approach to, and some achievement of, the defined attribute in the assessed process. Some aspects of achievement of the attribute may be unpredictable. - 15%-50% achievement.
L = Largely achieved	- There is evidence of a systematic approach to, and significant achievement of, the defined attribute in the assessed process. Some weakness related to this attribute may exist in the assessed process. - 50%-85% achievement.
F = Fully achieved	- There is evidence of a complete and systematic approach to, and full achievement of, the defined attribute in the assessed process. No significant weaknesses related to this attribute exist in the assessed process. - 85%-100% achievement.

Chapter 6 - Implementing COBIT 5

The purpose of this chapter is to highlight a number of important topics from the *COBIT 5 Implementation Guide* and some considerations for the implementation of COBIT.

ISACA provides practical and extensive implementation guidance in its publication *COBIT 5 Implementation* which is based on a continual improvement lifecycle. It is not intended to be a prescriptive approach or a complete solution, but rather a guide to avoid commonly encountered pitfalls. The guide is also supported by an implementation tool kit containing a variety of resources that are continually improved by ISACA.

The need to implement a Governance Enterprise IT (GEIT) program is triggered by specific internal and external factors within the enterprise environment. And its subsequent implementation will take place under different conditions and circumstances. Every enterprise needs to design its own road map considering these factors, conditions and circumstances. Internal and external factors that must be considered are:
- The community's ethics and culture
- Ruling laws, regulations and policies (legal, industry and government)
- The enterprise:
  - Mission, vision, goals and values
  - Governance policies and practices
  - Culture and management style
  - Models for roles and responsibilities
  - Business plans and strategic intentions
  - Operating model and level of maturity

It is equally important to consider critical success factors for a successful implementation:
- Top management providing the direction and mandate for the initiative.
- Visible ongoing commitment and support.
- All parties supporting the governance and management processes.
- Effective communication and change enablement.
- Focusing on quick wins.
- Prioritizing the most beneficial improvements that are easiest to implement.

Identifying pain points and trigger events at early stages will contribute to create a sense of urgency of the need to implement Governance Enterprise IT (GEIT) or to improve the existing program.

> A *pain point* is a problem that is or has been perceived.
> An *trigger event* is an occurrence that creates an opportunity for Governance Enterprise IT.

This table lists common pain points and trigger events:

Pain points	Trigger events
• Business frustration with failed initiatives, rising IT costs and a perception of low business value. • Outsourcing service delivery problems, such as consistent failure to meet agreed-on service levels. • Duplication or overlap between initiatives, projects or wasting resources. • IT-enabled changes failing to meet business needs. • Board and top management reluctant to engage with IT.	• Merger, acquisition or divestiture. • New regulatory or compliance requirements. • A significant technology change. • An enterprise-wide governance focus. • A new business strategy.

COBIT 5 Implementation Lifecycle

The COBIT 5 implementation lifecycle consists of <u>seven</u> phases that can be used for a successful implementation ensuring that nothing is left. Key aspects and activities are grouped by phase. Each phase has three key components that are interrelated. Figure 20 illustrates the lifecycle approach for the implementation of COBIT 5.

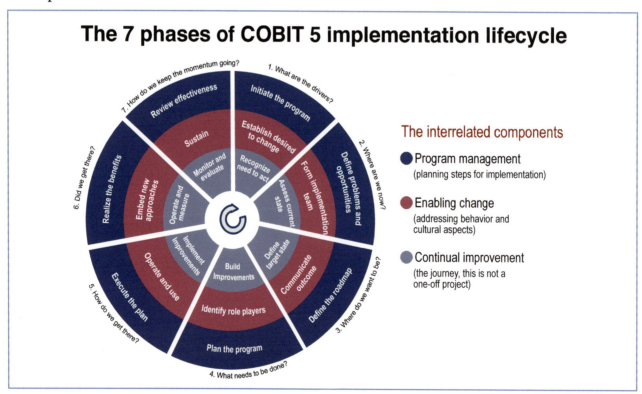

Figure 20 - Reproduced under permission of ISACA. All rights reserved.

Each phase has specific activities that are summarized in this table:

Phase	Key activities
1 - *What are the drivers?*	• Recognize the need to improve. • Identify pain points. • Identify trigger events. • Create a desire to change.
2 - *Where are we now?*	• Define the implementation scope by mapping enterprise goals to IT-related goals. • Map the IT-related goals to processes. • Analyze risks and prioritize improvements. • Perform assessment of current state ('as-is').

3 - *Where do we want to be?*	• Set the improvement target ('to-be').
	• Perform gap analysis.
	• Prioritize the potential solutions:
	  • Quick-wins
	  • Greatest benefits
	  • Easier to achieve

4 - *What needs to be done?*	• Prepare and present the business case based on the practical solutions that have been identified. • Develop the implementation plan to enable the change.
5 - *How do we get there?*	• Implement proposed solutions into day-to-day practices. • Measure and monitor to ensure alignment with business needs. • Engage stakeholders.
6 - *Did we get there?*	• Monitor achievement of expected outcomes. • Focus on sustaining the operation of new enablers.
7 - *How do we keep the momentum going?*	• Review the overall success of the improvement initiative. • Identify further improvements for the governance and management of enterprise IT. • Reinforce the need for continual improvement.

The implementation and improvement program should be continual and iterative. During the last phase, new objectives and requirements may arise and a new cycle should be initiated. Previous health checks, assessments and audits often trigger consideration of a GEIT initiative and these results can be used as input to phase 1.

Making the business case

To ensure the success of implementation initiatives leveraging COBIT, an appropriate level of urgency needs to be instilled and the key stakeholders should be aware of the risk of 'doing nothing' as well as the benefits of committing to the program. The initiative should be owned by a sponsor and should involve all key stakeholders. The proposed improvement must be justified on the basis of its expected benefits for the enterprise. It is documented and communicated through a business case.

> A *business case* is decision-making tool used to understand the effects that the particular improvement will have.

The business case should include expected benefits, critical tasks and milestones as well as key roles and responsibilities. Bear in mind that this is not a one-time static document, but a dynamic operational tool that must be continually reviewed and updated.

A good business case describes:
- The targeted business benefits.
- The required business changes for a successful implementation.
- The investment with estimated initial and ongoing costs.
- The associated risks, constraints and dependencies.
- Roles and responsibilities.
- How value creation will be measured and monitor.

Appendix A - COBIT 5 Enterprise Goals

BSC Dimension	Enterprise goal	Relation to Governance Objective		
		Benefits realization	Risk optimization	Resources optimization
Financial	1. Stakeholder value of business investments	P		S
	2. Portfolio of competitive products and services	P	P	S
	3. Managed business risk (safeguarding of assets)		P	S
	4. Compliance with external laws and regulations		P	
	5. Financial transparency	P	S	S
Customer	6. Customer-oriented service culture	P		S
	7. Business service continuity and availability		P	
	8. Agile responses to a changing business environment	P		S
	9. Information-based strategic decision making	P	P	P
	10. Optimization of service delivery costs	P		P
Internal	11. Optimization of business process functionality	P		P
	12. Optimization of business process costs	P		P
	13. Managed business change programs	P	P	S
	14. Operational and staff productivity	P		P
	15. Compliance with internal policies		P	
Learning	16. Skilled and motivated people	S	P	P
	17. Product and business innovation culture	P		

Appendix B - Mapping Enterprise Goals to IT-related Goals

Enterprise Goals to IT-related Goals - Reproduced under permission of ISACA. All rights reserved.
THE LEAN IT GROUP, LLC - COBIT 5 FOUNDATION CCOURSE's Toolbox

Enterprise Goals:

#	Category	Enterprise Goal
1	Financial	Stakeholder value of business investments
2	Financial	Portfolio of competitive products and services
3	Financial	Managed business risk (safeguarding of assets)
4	Financial	Compliance with external laws and regulations
5	Financial	Financial transparency
6	Customer	Customer-oriented service culture
7	Customer	Business service continuity and availability
8	Customer	Agile responses to a changing business environment
9	Customer	Information-based strategic decision making
10	Internal	Optimization of service delivery costs
11	Internal	Optimization of business process functionality
12	Internal	Optimization of business process costs
13	Internal	Managed business change programmes
14	Internal	Operational and staff productivity
15	Internal	Compliance with internal policies
16	Learning/Growth	Skilled and motivated people
17	Learning/Growth	Product and business innovation culture

IT-related Goals mapped to Enterprise Goals (P = Primary, S = Secondary):

IT-related Goal	1	2	3	4	5	6	7	8	9	10	11	12	13	14	15	16	17
1. Alignment of IT and business strategy (Financial)	P	P	S			P	S	P	P	S	P	S	P			S	S
2. IT compliance and support for business compliance with external laws and regulations (Financial)		S	S	P											P		
3. Commitment of executive management for making IT-related decisions (Financial)	P	S	P	S			P	S	S	P	S		S		S	S	S
4. Managed IT-related business risk (Financial)	P		P	S	P		S								S		
5. Realized benefits from IT-enabled investments and services portfolio (Financial)	P	P			P	S					S	S	S				S
6. Transparency of IT costs, benefits and risk (Financial)	S		S		P												
7. Delivery of IT services in line with business requirements (Customer)	P	P	S	S		P	S	S	S	P	P	P	S	S		S	S
8. Adequate use of applications, information and technology solutions (Customer)	S		S			S	S			S	P	S	S	P		S	S
9. IT agility (Customer)	S					S		P		S	P	S	S	S		S	P
10. Security of information, processing infrastructure and applications (Internal)		S	P	P			P								S		
11. Optimization of IT assets, resources and capabilities (Internal)	P	S	S					S		P	S	P	S	P		S	S
12. Enablement and support of business processes by integrating applications and technology into business processes (Internal)	S	P	S			S		S		S	P	S	S	S			S
13. Delivery of programmes delivering benefits, on time, on budget, and meeting requirements and quality standards (Internal)	P	S				S				S	P		P				
14. Availability of reliable and useful information for decision making (Internal)	S		S		S		P		P			S		S			
15. IT compliance with internal policies (Internal)				S											P		
16. Competent and motivated business and IT personnel (Learning/Growth)	S		S											P		P	S
17. Knowledge, expertise and initiatives for business innovation (Learning/Growth)	S	P				S		S	P		P	S	S	S		S	P

Appendix C - Mapping IT-related Goals to COBIT 5 Processes

COBIT 5 Processes			1. Alignment of IT and business strategy	2. IT compliance and support for business compliance with external laws and regulations.	3. Commitment of executive management for making IT-related decisions.	4. Managed IT-related business risk.	5. Realized benefits from IT-enabled investments and services portfolio.	6. Transparency of IT costs, benefits and risk.	7. Delivery of IT services in line with business requirements.	8. Adequate use of applications, information and technology solutions.	9. IT agility	10. Security of information, processing infrastructure and applications	11. Optimization of IT assets, resources and capabilities.	12. Enablement and support of business processes by integrating applications and technology into business processes	13. Delivery of programmes delivering benefits, on time, on budget, and meeting requirements and quality standards.	14. Availability of reliable and useful information for decision making.	15. IT compliance with internal policies.	16. Competent and motivated business and IT personnel.	17. Knowledge, expertise and initiatives for business innovation.
		IT-related goals	**Financial**						**Customer**			**Internal**						**Learning/Growth**	
EDM	01	Ensure Governance Framework Setting and Maintenance	P	S	P	S	S	S	P	S	S	S	S	S	S	S	S	S	S
	02	Ensure Benefits Delivery	P		S	S	P	P	P	S			S		S	S	S		P
	03	Ensure Risk Optimization	S	S	S	P		P	S	S	P	P	P		S	S	P	S	S
	04	Ensure Resource Optimization	S		P	S	S	S	S	S	P		P					P	S
	05	Ensure Stakeholder Transparency	S	S	P	S	S	P	S				P			S	S		S
APO	01	Manage the IT Management Framework	P		S	S	S	S	P	S	P	S	P	S	S	S	P	P	P
	02	Manage Strategy	P		S	S	S	S	S	S	P		S	S		S	S	S	P
	03	Manage Enterprise Architecture	P		S	S	P	S	S	P	P	S	P	S	P	S	S		P
	04	Manage Innovation	S		S	S	P	S	S	P	P		P	S	P	S		P	P
	05	Manage Portfolio	P		S	S	P	S	S	S	S		P	P	P	S			S
	06	Manage Budget and Costs	S			S	P	P	S		S		P						
	07	Manage Human Resources	P			S	S	S	P	S	S	S	S	P	S	P	S	P	P
	08	Manage Relationships	P		S	S	S	P	P	S	S		S	P	S	S	S	S	P
	09	Manage Service Agreements	S			P	P	P	P	S	S	S	S	S	P	P	S	S	S
	10	Manage Suppliers		S		P	S	P	P	S	S	S	S		S	S	S		S
	11	Manage Quality	S	S		P		P	S	S	P		S		P	S	S	S	S
	12	Manage Risk		P		P		P	S		S	P	S		P	S	S	S	S
	13	Manage Security		P		P			S		S	P				P	S	S	S

THE LEAN IT GROUP, LLC - COBIT 5 FOUNDATION CCOURSE's Toolbox
IT-related Goals to Processes - Reproduced under permission of ISACA. All rights reserved.

Appendix C - Mapping IT-related Goals to COBIT 5 Processes

COBIT 5 Processes		1. Alignment of IT and business strategy	2. IT compliance and support for business compliance with external laws and regulations	3. Commitment of executive management for making IT-related decisions	4. Managed IT-related business risk	5. Realized benefits from IT-enabled investments and services portfolio	6. Transparency of IT costs, benefits and risk	7. Delivery of IT services in line with business requirements	8. Adequate use of applications, information and technology solutions	9. IT agility	10. Security of information, processing infrastructure and applications	11. Optimization of IT assets, resources and capabilities	12. Enablement and support of business processes by integrating applications and technology into business processes	13. Delivery of programmes delivering benefits, on time, on budget, and meeting requirements and quality standards	14. Availability of reliable and useful information for decision making	15. IT compliance with internal policies	16. Competent and motivated business and IT personnel	17. Knowledge, expertise and initiatives for business innovation
	IT-related goals →	Financial	Financial	Financial	Financial	Financial	Financial	Customer	Customer	Customer	Internal	Internal	Internal	Internal	Internal	Internal	Learning/Growth	Learning/Growth
BAI 01	Manage Programmes and Projects	P		S	P	P	S	S	S			S		P			S	S
BAI 02	Manage Requirements Definition	P	S	S	S	S		P	S	S	S	S	P	S	S			S
BAI 03	Manage Solutions Identification and Build	S			S	S		P	S	S		S	S	S	S			S
BAI 04	Manage Availability and Capacity	S			S	S		P	P	S	P	P	S		P			P
BAI 05	Manage Organizational Change Enablement					S		S	P	S		S	S	P				S
BAI 06	Manage Changes			S	P	S		P	P	S	S		P	S	S	S		S
BAI 07	Manage Change Acceptance and Transitioning				S	S		S	S	P	S	S		S	S	S		P
BAI 08	Manage Knowledge	S	S				P			S	S	P					S	
BAI 09	Manage Assets		P		S	S	S	P	S	S	S	P			P	S		S
BAI 10	Manage Configuration		S		S	S			S			P			S	S		S
DSS 01	Manage Operations				P			P	S	S	S					S		S
DSS 02	Manage Service Requests and Incidents				P	S		P	S	S		P	S		P	S		
DSS 03	Manage Problems	S	S		P			P	S			S	S		P	S		
DSS 04	Manage Continuity	S	S		P			P				S	S		S	S	S	
DSS 05	Manage Security Services		P		P			S			S				S	S		
DSS 06	Manage Business Process Controls		S		P			P							S	S	S	S

THE LEAN IT GROUP, LLC - COBIT 5 FOUNDATION CCOURSE's Toolbox
IT-related Goals to Processes - Reproduced under permission of ISACA. All rights reserved.

Appendix C - Mapping IT-related Goals to COBIT 5 Processes

COBIT 5 Processes			Financial					Customer			Internal						Learning/Growth	
		IT-related goals	1. Alignment of IT and business strategy	2. IT compliance and support for business compliance with external laws and regulations.	3. Commitment of executive management for making IT-related decisions.	4. Managed IT-related business risk.	5. Realized benefits from IT-enabled investments and services portfolio.	6. Transparency of IT costs, benefits and risk.	7. Delivery of IT services in line with business requirements.	8. Adequate use of applications, information and technology solutions.	9. IT agility	10. Security of information, processing infrastructure and applications	11. Optimization of IT assets, resources and capabilities.	12. Enablement and support of business processes by integrating applications and technology into business processes	13. Delivery of programmes delivering benefits, on time, on budget, and meeting requirements and quality standards.	14. Availability of reliable and useful information for decision making.	15. IT compliance with internal policies.	16. Competent and motivated business and IT personnel.	17. Knowledge, expertise and initiatives for business innovation.
MEA	01	Monitor, Evaluate and Assess Performance and Conformance	S	S	S	P	S	S	P	S	S	S	P		S	S	P	S	S
	02	Monitor, Evaluate and Assess the System of Internal Control		P		P		S	S	S		S				S	P		S
	03	Monitor, Evaluate and Assess Compliance With External Requirements		P		P	S		S	S		S					S		S

THE LEAN IT GROUP, LLC - COBIT 5 FOUNDATION CCOURSE's Toolbox
IT-related Goals to Processes - Reproduced under permission of ISACA. All rights reserved.

Appendix D
COBIT 5 - Governance and Management Interactions

Enabler	Interaction
Processes	A distinction is made between governance and management processes, including specific sets of practices and activities for each. The process model also includes RACI charts, describing the responsibilities of different organisational structures and roles within the enterprise.
Information	The process model describes inputs to and outputs from the different process practices to other processes, including information exchanged between governance and management processes. Information used for evaluating, directing and monitoring enterprise IT is exchanged between governance and management as described in the process model inputs and outputs.
Organizational structures	A number of organisational structures are defined in each enterprise; structures can sit in the governance space or the management space, depending on their composition and scope of decisions. Because governance is about setting the direction, interaction takes place between the decisions taken by the governance structures—e.g., deciding about the investment portfolio and setting risk appetite—and the decisions and operations implementing the former.
Principles, policies and frameworks	Principles, policies and frameworks are the vehicle by which governance decisions are institutionalised within the enterprise, and for that reason are an interaction between governance decisions (direction setting) and management (execution of decisions).
Culture, ethics and behavior	Behavior is also a key enabler of good governance and management of the enterprise. It is set at the top—leading by example—and is therefore an important interaction between governance and management.
People, skills and competencies	Governance and management activities require different skill sets, but an essential skill for both governance body members and management is to understand both tasks and how they are different.
Services, infrastructure and applications	Services are required, supported by applications and infrastructure to provide the governance body with adequate information and to support the governance activities of evaluating, setting direction and monitoring.

Appendix E
COBIT 5 - Organizational Structures Matrix

ROLE	DESCRIPTION
Board	The group of the most senior executives and/or non-executive directors of the enterprise who are accountable for the governance of the enterprise and have overall control of its resources.
CEO	The highest-ranking officer who is in charge of the total management of the enterprise.
CFO	The most senior official of the enterprise who is accountable for all aspects of financial management, including financial risk and controls and reliable and accurate accounts.
COO	The most senior official of the enterprise who is accountable for the operation of the enterprise.
CRO	The most sen or official of the enterprise who is accountable for all aspects of risk management across the enterprise. An IT risk officer function may be established to oversee IT-related risk.
CIO	The most senior official of the enterprise who is responsible for aligning IT and business strategies and accountable for planning, resourcing and managing the delivery of IT services and solutions to support enterprise objectives.
CISO	The most senior official of the enterprise who is accountable for the security of enterprise information in all its forms.
Business Executive	A senior management individual accountable for the operation of a specific business unit or subsidiary.
Business Process Owner	An individual accountable for the performance of a process in realizing its objectives, driving process improvement and approving process changes.
Strategy IT Committee	A group of senior executives appointed by the board to ensure that the board is involved in, and kept informed of, major IT-related matters and decisions. The committee is accountable for managing the portfolios of IT-enabled investments, IT services and IT assets, ensuring that value is delivered and risk is managed. The committee is normally chaired by a board member, not by the CIO.
Project/Program Steering Committee	A group of stakeholders and experts who are accountable for guidance of programmes and projects, including management and monitoring of plans, allocation of resources, delivery of benefits and value, and management of programme and project risk.
Architecture Board	A group of stakeholders and experts who are accountable for guidance on enterprise architecture-related matters and decisions, and for setting architectural policies and standards.
Enterprise Risk Committee	The group of executives of the enterprise who are accountable for the enterprise-level collaboration and consensus required to support enterprise risk management (ERM) activities and decisions. An IT risk council may be established to consider IT risk in more detail and advise the enterprise risk committee.

Appendix E
COBIT 5 - Organizational Structures Matrix

Head of HR	The most senior official of an enterprise who is accountable for planning and policies with respect to all human resources in that enterprise.
Compliance	The function in the enterprise responsible for guidance on legal, regulatory and contractual compliance.
Audit	The function in the enterprise responsible for provision of internal audits.
Head of Architecture	A senior individual accountable for the enterprise architecture process.
Head of Development	A senior individual accountable for IT-related solution development processes.
Head of IT Operations	A senior individual accountable for the IT operational environments and infrastructure.
Head of IT Administration	A senior individual accountable for IT-related records and responsible for supporting IT-related administrative matters.
Program/Project Management Office (PMO)	The function responsible for supporting programme and project managers, and gathering, assessing and reporting information about the conduct of their programmes and constituent projects.
Value Management Office (VMO)	The function that acts as the secretariat for managing investment and service portfolios, including assessing and advising on investment opportunities and business cases, recommending value governance/management methods and controls, and reporting on progress on sustaining and creating value from investments and services.
Service Manager	An individual who manages the development, implementation, evaluation and ongoing management of new and existing products and services for a specific customer (user) or group of customers (users).
Information Security Management	An individual who manages, designs, oversees and/or assesses an enterprise's information security.
Business Continuity Management	An individual who manages, designs, oversees and/or assesses an enterprise's business continuity capability, to ensure that the enterprise's critical functions continue to operate following disruptive events.
Privacy Officer	An individual who is responsible for monitoring the risk and business impacts of privacy laws and for guiding and coordinating the implementation of policies and activities that will ensure that the privacy directives are met. Also called data protection officer.

Appendix F
COBIT 5 - Information Quality Categories

COBIT 4.1	COBIT 5 Quality goals	DESCRIPTION
Effectiveness	Appropriate amount Relevance Understandability Interpretability Objectivity	Information is effective if it meets the needs of the information consumer who uses the information for a specific task. If the information consumer can perform the task with the information, then the information is effective.
Efficiency	Believability Accessibility Ease of operation Reputation	Whereas effectiveness considers the information as a product, efficiency relates more to the process of obtaining and using information, so it aligns to the 'information as a service' view. If information that meets the needs of the information consumer is obtained and used in an easy way, then the use of information is efficient.
Integrity	Completeness Accuracy	If information has integrity, then it is free of error and complete.
Reliability	Believability Reputation Objectivity	Reliability is often seen as a synonym of accuracy; however, it can also be said that information is reliable if it is regarded as true and credible. Compared to integrity, reliability is more subjective, more related to perception, and not just factual.
Availability	Availability	Availability is one of the information quality goals under the accessibility and security heading.
Confidentiality	Confidentiality	Confidentiality corresponds to the restricted access information quality goal.
Compliance	Compliance	Compliance in the sense that information must conform to specifications is covered by any of the information quality goals, depending on the requirements. Compliance to regulations is most often a goal or requirement of the use of the information, not so much an inherent quality of information.

Appendix G
COBIT 5 - Skill Categories

Process domain	Skill category
Evaluate, Direct and Monitor (EDM)	- Governance of enterprise IT
Align, Plan and Organise (APO)	- IT policy formulation - IT strategy - Enterprise architecture - Innovation - Financial management - Portfolio management
Build, Acquire and Implement (BAI)	- Business analysis - Project management - Usability evaluation - Requirements definition and management - Programming - System ergonomics - Software decommissioning - Capacity management
Deliver, Service and Support (DSS)	- Availability management - Problem management - Service desk and incident management - Security administration - IT operations - Database administration
Monitor, Evaluate and Assess (MEA)	- Compliance review - Performance monitoring - Controls audit

APPENDIX H
COBIT 5 - Process Reference Model

Governance processes

Evaluate, direct and monitor (EDM) - To establish the stakeholders governance objectives

EDM01 - Ensure Governance Framework Setting and Maintenance	EDM02 - Ensure Benefits Delivery	EDM03 - Ensure Risk Optimization	EDM04 - Ensure Resource Optimization	EDM05 - Ensure Stakeholders Transparency

Management processes

Align, plan and organize (APO) - To provide direction to solution and service delivery and for ongoing support

APO01 - Manage the IT Management Framework	APO02 - Manage Strategy	APO03 - Manage Enterprise Architecture	APO04 - Manage Innovation	APO05 - Manage Portfolio	APO06 - Manage Budget and Costs	APO07 - Manage Human Resources
APO08 - Manage Relationships	APO09 - Manage Service Agreements	APO10 - Manage Suppliers	APO11 - Manage Quality	APO12 - Manage Risk	APO13 - Manage Security	

Build, acquire and implement (BAI) - To turn solutions into valuable services

BAI01 - Manage Programmes and Projects	BAI02 - Manage Requirements Definition	BAI03 - Manage Solutions Identification and Build	BAI04 - Manage Availability and Capacity	BAI05 - Manage Organizational Change Enablement	BAI06 - Manage Changes	BAI07 - Manage Change Acceptance and Transitioning
BAI08 - Manage Knowledge	BAI09 - Manage Assets	BAI10 - Manage Configuration				

Deliver, service and support (DSS) - To make solutions usable for the end-users

DSS01 - Manage Operations	DSS02 - Manage Service Requests and Incidents	DSS03 - Manage Problems	DSS04 - Manage Continuity	DSS05 - Manage Security Services	DSS06 - Manage Business Process Controls	

Monitor, evaluate and assess (MEA) - Ensure direction is followed

MEA01 - Monitor, Evaluate and Assess Performance and Conformance	MEA02 - Monitor, Evaluate and Assess the System of Internal Control	MEA03 - Monitor, Evaluate and Assess Compliance With External Requirements

THE LEAN IT GROUP, LLC - COBIT 5 FOUNDATION COURSE's Toolbox
Reproduced under permission of ISACA. All rights reserved
COBiT is a registered trademark of ISACA registered in the United States and other countries

APPENDIX I
COBIT 5 - Process Capability Model

PROCESS CAPABILITY ASSESSMENT	
Capability Level	Attributes Required
Level 0 - Imcomplete	
Level 1 - Performed	PA 1.1
Level 2 - Managed	PA 1.1 PA 2.1 PA 2.2
Level 3 - Established	PA 1.1 PA 2.1 PA 2.2 PA 3.1 PA 3.2
Level 4 - Predictable	PA 1.1 PA 2.1 PA 2.2 PA 3.1 PA 3.2 PA 4.1 PA 4.2
Level 5 - Optimizing	PA 1.1 PA 2.1 PA 2.2 PA 3.1 PA 3.2 PA 4.1 PA 4.2 PA 5.1 PA 5.2

PROCESS CAPABILITY ATTRIBUTES - ISO/IEC 15504		
Attribute ID	Attribute Name	Description
PA 1.1	Process performance	The implemented process achieves its process purpose.
PA 2.1	Performance management	A measure of the extent to which the performance of the process is managed.
PA 2.2	Work product management	A measure of the extent to which the work products produced by the process are appropriately managed. The work products (or outputs from the process) are defined and controlled.
PA 3.1	Process definition	A measure of the extent to which a standard process is maintained to support the deployment of the defined process.
PA 3.2	Process deployment	A measure of the extent to which the standard process is effectively deployed as a defined process to achieve its process outcomes.
PA 4.1	Process measurement	A measure of the extent to which measurement results are used to ensure that performance of the process supports the achievement of relevant process performance objectives in support of defined business goals.
PA 4.2	Process control	A measure of the extent to which the process is quantitatively managed to produce a process that is stable, capable and predictable within defined limits.
PA 5.1	Process innovation	A measure of the extent to which changes to the process are identified from analysis of common causes of variation in performance, and from investigations of innovative approaches to the definition and deployment of the process.
PA 5.2	Process optimization	A measure of the extent to which changes to the definition, management and performance of the process result in effective impact that achieves the relevant process improvement objectives

Each attribute is rated using a standard rating scale defined in the ISO/IEC 15504 standard as shown below.

Abbreviation	Description	% Achieved
N	Not achieved	0 to 15% achievement
P	Partially achieved	>15% to 50% achievement
L	Largely achieved	>50% to 85% achievement
F	Fully achieved	>85% to 100% achievement

THE LEAN IT GROUP, LLC - COBIT 5 FOUNDATION COURSE's Toolbox
Reproduced under permission of ISACA. All rights reserved
COBIT is a registered trademark of ISACA registered in the United States and other countries

Appendix J - Feetwalk Case Study for COBIT 5 Foundation Course

Company background

Joseph Murano founded FeetWalk Store in 1999, as a result of his frustration finding the right size, color, and style of shoe. After trying several stores, he felt there must be a better way. Stores carried a relatively small selection of styles, and usually did not have a full complement of colors and sizes even for the styles they did stock. This was not surprising considering the physical constraints of shoe stores, the limited number of shoes that an average store would stock, and the small local population served by individual stores.

The Internet era was in full swing. Mr. Murano realized that what consumers needed was a way to access a huge selection of styles, colors, and sizes. Since none existed, Murano decided to create one, using the Internet to address the selection problems faced by traditional shoe retailers—despite having no experience in retail, let alone the shoe industry.

Feetwalk Store began in San Francisco, in the second floor of a Victorian house. By 2004, the company needed to expand, with particular emphasis on its call center. The senior management believed that it was important to have the call center as part of corporate headquarters, rather than outsource or remotely locate this function—after all, the company's primary focus was on providing the very best customer experience, and the call center was central to achieving this objective. The Bay Area was expensive, but it also did not have the right environment, neither access to suitable employees to staff the type of call center that they believed was essential to the company's success.

They decided to move Feetwalk Store to Henderson, Nevada, USA, on the outskirts of Las Vegas. Las Vegas is a service-oriented city that operates on a 24-7 schedule, was already home to many call centers, and has extremely good Internet connectivity. Of the 90 employees in San Francisco, 70 moved to Las Vegas.

Today, Feetwalk has become a $1 billion retailer and reported net income of $10.8 million. The company employs 1,200 employees in its Nevada office: 300 in its call center, 250 in retailing, 385 in the fulfillment center and the balance in supporting departments including IT.

Company's brands

Feetwalk Store focused its attention on signing brands that customers searched for or asked for when talking to call center representatives. The company reviewed logs of customer searches for brands that were not on its site, and its buyers investigated those brands and evaluated whether they would be valuable additions to Feetwalk Store offering. As the company grew and became well known within the industry, brands began to contact Feetwalk Store about being sold through the site. As Steve Montana, the vice president of Retailing said, "[The buyer] will get in touch with the brand, talk to them, and look at the product. If there's a compelling reason to have the product, then we'll go ahead and open the brand. In a lot of cases, it would be duplication of something we already have, so we may not go down that road."

COPYRIGHT © THE LEAN IT GROUP, LLC. All rights reserved.

Appendix J - Feetwalk Case Study for COBIT 5 Foundation Course

High-end brands, initially reluctant to partner with online retailers such as Feetwalk Store, eventually came on board for several reasons. First, as consumers became comfortable buying online, this became an important distribution channel. Second, they began to realize that if customers could not purchase authentic high-end brands, it made it easier for counterfeiters—customers searching for their brands on the Internet would end up on sites that sold fakes.

The challenges

Global Economy - while high-end brick-and-mortar retailers reported double-digit sales decreases in past fiscal year, Feetwalk continues to grow, although at a somewhat slower rate. Margins are decreasing, however. The changing economy poses challenges on many fronts. In looking at how best to prepare for difficult economic times, the company is looking at all aspects of its business for improvements and efficiencies, including its supply chain.

Delivery Schedules - another challenge is the limited visibility into the manufacturers' supply chains, and there is a high degree of uncertainty as to the actual day that a shipment will arrive at the warehouse.

Excessive inventory - Feetwalk does not want its success to be based on discounting. The basic operating principle of the company is to deliver the very best service. Thus, with respect to disposing of excess inventory, the primary focus should be based on the buying decision. Feetwalk wants to have the right products, in the right quantities, at the right time. However, it is inevitable that there be some excess inventory.

Corporate values

From the beginning, Feetwalk set out to provide an exceptional shopping experience for its customers. It wants customers, after any interaction with the company, to say "Wow!" Anything to improve customer service is considered an investment rather than an expense.

The drive to provide a "wow experience" extends to every aspect of the company. The Feetwalk website loads faster than any other retail website. While most orders are made online, telephone support is essential for maximizing the customer experience. Unlike other popular retail sites, the company's toll-free phone number is prominently displayed on all its web pages, the average phone call is answered in less than 30 seconds, and call center representatives has the authority to resolve virtually any issue.

Everyone is focused on just being the very best at whatever particular department he or she is in. It is definitely a thread that runs throughout the company. It's a lifestyle. They're always living, breathing, and thinking about the company. After work, people don't go home and forget about what happened at Feetwalk. They go out with other Feetwalk employees, and they have

Appendix J - Feetwalk Case Study for COBIT 5 Foundation Course

fun, they bond and build relationships, but they're always talking about, 'How can we move the business forward? How can we innovate? How can we make it better?'

Feetwalk has a strong feedback program in which employees and partners participate besides customers. The feedback program is managed by the Quality and Excellence Department. The program is based on the following corporate core values:

1. Deliver WOW Through Service
2. Embrace and Drive Change
3. Pursue Growth and Learning
4. Build Open and Honest Relationships
5. Do More with Less

Powered by Feetwalk

The company's vision *"To be the premier online retailer with the best service and best selection"* is about to change. Due to economy downturn, Feetwalk's growth has slowed down due primarily to an increased competition and decreased margins. The changing economy poses challenges on many fronts. In looking at how best to prepare for difficult economic times, the company has identified a niche market: small to medium-sized manufacturing companies that want to sell their products online directly to end-customers. To do this, they need to develop websites to sell products, and a distribution network to deliver products directly to customers—in small shipments to large numbers of destinations. The companies would have to develop several areas of competence: the technology to design and run a retail website, a call center to deal with customer questions and problems, and a distribution system optimized for delivery to retail customers.

These are all areas in which Feetwalk excels. They have an enviable IT infrastructure that, for many years, has proven to be very reliable, stable and sophisticated. It is continually improved to ensure high availability and business continuity. The IT infrastructure is considered a critical asset for the business.

To serve this niche market, Marketing and Retailing management has created a new business concept: ***"Powered by Feetwalk"***. Under this concept, Feetwalk will develop and run the website for the potential manufacturers, will run their call center and will distribute directly to their end-customers. Suppose the manufacturer is the hypothetical "Smith Leathers", customers will go to the company website, http://www.smithleathers.com, which will display their products. The http://www.smithleathers.com will include a prominent ***"Powered by Feetwalk"*** logo. The customer orders a product, and the order is sent to the Feetwalk's distribution center, where it is handled just like any other order. Customers that have a question or problem call the number on the http://www.smithleathers.com, which is answered by an operator at the Feetwalk's call center. Smith Leathers pays Feetwalk to develop and run the website, and to handle its customers at the call center. Feetwalk will keep a consignment inventory of these

Appendix J - Feetwalk Case Study for COBIT 5 Foundation Course

manufacturers and will purchase the sold items at wholesale prices, and sell them to the customer at retail prices.

With the implementation of *"Powered by Feetwalk"* the company will face three key challenges.
1. Delivering the WOW experience to potential manufacturers and their end-customers while delivering the same experience to Feetwalk's end-customers.
2. Complying with new regulations and information security requirements.
3. Ensuring business continuity and high available services.

Organizational structure

There are five key areas reporting to the CEO. The CEO and the vice-presidents comprise the Executive Board:
- Retailing – focused on retail services, product strategy and business relationships with suppliers and partners. Responsible for the Quality and Excellence Program. Recently, a Project Management Office (PMO) was established reporting to Retailing.
- Marketing – responsible for www.feetwalk.com customer-facing side. Also responsible for the media advertising, affiliates network development, social media, email marketing, event sponsorships etc.
- Human Resources (HR) – recruiting, employee's compensation plans, training and new-hire program.
- Finance – Account Payables, Account Receivables, budgeting, forecasting and auditing. Responsible for outsourced services: Payroll and Risk Management.
- Operations – responsible for the Fulfillment Center operation, call center and IT.

Appendix J - Feetwalk Case Study for COBIT 5 Foundation Course

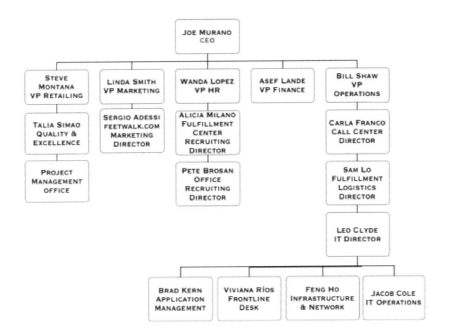

Appendix K - AnswerKey to Practices

Chapter 2

Practice - The Goals cascade

Enterprise goals		IT-related-goals	
4	Compliance with external laws and regulations	2	IT compliance and support for business compliance with external laws and regulations.
		10	Security of information, processing infrastructure and applications.
6	Customer-oriented service culture.	1	Alignment of IT and business strategy.
		7	Delivery of IT services in line with business requirements.
7	Business service continuity and availability.	4	Managed IT-related business risk.
		10	Security of information, processing infrastructure and applications.
		14	Availability of reliable and useful information for decision making.

Chapter 3

Practice - Mapping IT-related goals to COBIT 5 processes

IT-related-goals		COBIT 5 Processes	
2	IT compliance and support for business compliance with external laws and regulations.	APO01 APO12 APO13 BAI10 DSS05 MEA02 MEA03	Manage the IT management framework Manage risk Manage security Manage configuration Manage security services Monitor, evaluate, and assess the system of internal control Monitor, evaluate, and assess compliance with external requirements.
10	Security of information, processing infrastructure and applications.	EDM03 APO12 APO13 BAI06	Ensure risk optimization Manage risk Manage security Manage changes

Appendix K - AnswerKey to Practices

1	Alignment of IT and business strategy.	EDM01	Ensure governance framework setting and maintenance
		EDM02	Ensure benefits delivery
		APO01	Manage the IT management framework
		APO02	Manage strategy
		APO03	Manage enterprise architecture
		APO05	Manage portfolio
		APO07	Manage human resources
		APO08	Manage relationships
		BAI01	Manage programs and projects
		BAI02	Manage requirements definition
7	Delivery of IT services in line with business requirements.	EDM01	Ensure governance framework setting and maintenance
		EDM02	Ensure benefits delivery
		EDM05	Ensure stakeholder transparency
		APO08	Manage relationships
		APO09	Manage service agreements
		APO10	Manage suppliers
		APO11	Manage quality
		BAI02	Manage requirements definition
		BAI03	Manage solutions identification and build
		BAI04	Manage availability and capacity
		BAI06	Manage changes
		DSS01	Manage operations
		DSS02	Manage service requests and incidents
		DSS03	Manage problems
		DSS04	Manage continuity
		DSS06	Manage business process controls
		MEA01	Monitor, evaluate, and assess performance and conformance
4	Managed IT-related business risk.	EDM03	Ensure risk optimization
		APO10	Manage suppliers
		APO12	Manage risk
		APO13	Manage security
		BAI01	Manage programs and projects
		BAI06	Manage changes
		DSS01	Manage operations
		DSS02	Manage service requests and incidents
		DSS03	Manage problems
		DSS04	Manage continuity
		DSS05	Manage security services
		DSS06	Manage business process controls
		MEA01	Monitor, evaluate, and assess performance and conformance

Appendix K - AnswerKey to Practices

		MEA02 MEA03	Monitor, evaluate, and assess the system of internal control Monitor, evaluate, and assess compliance with external requirements.
10	Security of information, processing infrastructure and applications.	EDM03 APO12 APO13 BAI06	Ensure risk optimization Manage risk Manage security Manage changes
14	Availability of reliable and useful information for decision making.	APO09 APO13 BAI04 BAI10 DSS03 DSS04	Manage service agreements Manage security Manage availability and capacity Manage configuration Manage problems Manage continuity

Process enablers

Domain	Process ID	Process name
Evaluate, Direct and Monitor (EDM)	01	Ensure governance framework setting and maintenance
	02	Ensure benefits delivery
	03	Ensure risk optimization
	05	Ensure stakeholder transparency
Align, Plan and Organize (APO)	01	Manage the IT management framework
	02	Manage strategy
	03	Manage enterprise architecture
	05	Manage portfolio
	07	Manage human resources
	08	Manage relationships
	09	Manage service agreements
	10	Manage suppliers
	11	Manage quality
	12	Manage risk
	13	Manage security
Build, Acquire and Implement (BAI)	01	Manage programs and projects
	02	Manage requirements definition
	03	Manage solutions identification and build
	04	Manage availability and capacity
	06	Manage changes

Appendix K - AnswerKey to Practices

Deliver, Service and Support (DSS)	01	Manage operations
	02	Manage service requests and incidents
	03	Manage problems
	04	Manage continuity
	05	Manage security services
	06	Manage business process controls
Monitor, Evaluate and Assess (MEA)	01	Monitor, evaluate and assess performance and conformance
	02	Monitor, evaluate and assess the system of internal control
	03	Monitor, evaluate and assess compliance with external requirements.

Practice - Organizational structures

Role	Person in charge
CIO	Leo Clyde - IT Director
Program/Project Management Office (PMO)	Project Management Office
Service Manager	Leo Clyde - IT Director
Information Security Management	Feng Ho - Infrastructure and Network
Business Continuity Management	Bill Shaw - VP of Operations

COBIT® 5 Foundation Exam

Sample Paper

Multiple Choice

Instructions

1. All 50 questions should be attempted.
2. All answers are to be marked on the answer sheet provided.
3. Please use a pencil and NOT ink to mark your answers on the Answer sheet provided. There is only one correct answer per question.
4. You have 40 minutes for this paper.
5. You must get 25 or more correct answers to pass.

Candidate Number:...

This is a blank page

1. Which question is valid to ask when establishing how to manage the enabler performance?

    A. Are good practices applied?

    B. Is security ensured?

    C. Are operations efficient?

    D. Is performance monitored?

2. What type of process goal is compliant with external rules?

    A. Intrinsic

    B. Business

    C. Contextual

    D. Accessibility and security

3. What is the Programme Management Phase in the Implementation Life Cycle called when practical solutions are supported by justifiable business cases?

    A. Build improvements

    B. Define road map

    C. Plan programme

    D. Initiate programme

4. What is the name given to an enterprise communication mechanism for corporate values and desired behaviour?

   A. Process outcomes

   B. Organisational structures

   C. Principles and policies

   D. Rules and norms

5. Which requirement describes 'contextual quality' in the Goals Enabler dimension?

   A. Outcomes should be relevant and complete

   B. Enablers are available when, and if, needed

   C. Enablers provide accurate, objective and reputable results

   D. Outcomes are secured

6. Which statement is correct about the three COBIT guides, (Process Assessment Model, Assessor Guide, Self-assessment Guide)?

   A. The Process Assessment Model (PAM) is assessed by the Assessor Guide

   B. The Program Assessment Model does NOT have any value without the Assessor Guide

   C. The Self-Assessment Guide is the same as the Assessor Guide, but used internally in an organisation

   D. The Self-Assessment Guide can be used to prepare for a formal Process Capability Assessment

7. Which element is a key component of the COBIT 5 Governance Approach?

   A. Stakeholder Transparency

   B. Evaluate, Direct and Monitor

   C. Plan, Build, Run and Monitor

   D. Governance Scope

8. Which activity is a good practice of operating principles within the organisation structures enabler?

   A. Publishing a schedule of Board meetings in advance

   B. Issuing the boundaries of the organisational structure's decision rights

   C. Defining the structure to delegate decision rights

   D. Documenting the decisions which the structure is authorised to take

9. What is the purpose of the policies element within the principles, policies and frameworks model?

   A. To be open and flexible

   B. To specify consequences of failing to comply

   C. To provide detailed guidance on how to put principles into practice

   D. To express the core values of the enterprise

10. Identify the missing word(s) in the following sentence.

    Process [?] is a process attribute for a Predictable process.

    A. innovation
    B. performance management
    C. assessment
    D. measurement

11. What do Processes produce as a result of their operation?

    A. RACI charts
    B. Cultural aspects
    C. Service capabilities
    D. Business goals

12. What is the MOST suitable process domain for skills such as Portfolio Management?

    A. Monitor, Evaluate and Assess (MEA)
    B. Deliver, Service and Support (DSS)
    C. Build, Acquire and Implement (BAI)
    D. Align, Plan and Organise (APO)

13. Which enabler translates desired behaviour into practical guidance?

    A. Culture, Ethics and Behaviour

    B. Services, Infrastructure and Applications

    C. Principles, Policies and Frameworks

    D. People, Skills and Competencies

14. What role is the most senior official of the enterprise who is responsible for aligning IT and business strategies?

    A. Business Executive

    B. Head of Architecture

    C. Chief Information Officer (CIO)

    D. Chief Operating Officer (COO)

15. Which driver influences Stakeholder needs?

    A. Good practices

    B. Contextual quality

    C. Lag indicators

    D. Regulatory environment

16. Which is an important vehicle for executing policies?
    A. Organisational structures
    B. Process practices
    C. Governance framework
    D. Rules and Norms

17. What role is responsible for monitoring activities to achieve enterprise objectives in the Governance Approach?
    A. Governing Body
    B. Operations
    C. Stakeholders
    D. Management

18. What term is used to describe projects that are duplicated which may indicate a need for improved governance of enterprise IT?
    A. Mergers and acquisitions
    B. Pain points
    C. Trigger events
    D. IT risk

19. What is the purpose of the Process Reference Model?

    A. To be the basis for the capability dimension which defines the rating method to conform to ISO15504

    B. To be the basis for the process dimension which outlines the structure of the 37 COBIT processes

    C. To be the basis for the process dimension which gives the specific process references on each capability level

    D. To contain the generic attributes for the levels two, three, four and five

20. In what sequence would the following occur in the COBIT 5 Process Reference Model?

    1. Build
    2. Direct
    3. Plan

    A. 2,3,1

    B. 1,2,3

    C. 2,1,3

    D. 3,1,2

21. Identify the missing words in the following sentence.

    Enterprise Architecture is considered a skill category for the [?] Process Domain.

    A. Evaluate, Direct and Monitor (EDM)

    B. Build, Acquire and Implement (BAI)

    C. Align, Plan and Organise (APO)

    D. Monitor, Evaluate and Assess (MEA)

22. What capability level is an established process?
    A. Level 1
    B. Level 2
    C. Level 3
    D. Level 6

23. What are IT-related outcomes, required to achieve enterprise goals, represented by?
    A. IT-related goals
    B. Enabler goals
    C. IT balanced scorecard
    D. Processes

24. What is a collection of practices influenced by the enterprise's policies and procedures that takes input from a number of sources, manipulates the inputs and produces outputs known as?
    A. Framework
    B. Policies
    C. Enablers
    D. Process

25. How is the Governance Objective of 'Value Creation' met?

   A. By realising benefits

   B. By optimising resources

   C. By optimising risk

   D. All of the above

26. What is the purpose of the principles element within the principles, policies and frameworks model?

   A. To be limited in number

   B. To express the core values of the enterprise

   C. To be open and flexible to ensure policies achieve the stated purpose

   D. To provide a logical flow for staff who have to comply with them

27. Why is a process capability assessment performed?

   A. To identify process improvement

   B. To make a cost-benefit analysis of the process

   C. To judge the quality of the people executing the process

   D. To define the metrics of the process

28. What are stakeholder needs cascaded into?

    A. IT-related goals

    B. Enterprise goals

    C. Process goals

    D. Risk Optimisation goals

29. Which characteristic is necessary for a good policy?

    A. Effective

    B. Expresses the core values of the enterprise

    C. Intrusive

    D. Limited in number

30. What rating level must a process attain in order to pass an assessment?

    A. F - Only Fully

    B. P - Partially and or L - Largely

    C. L - Largely and or F - Fully

    D. P - Partially

31. Which action is a good practice to help encourage desired behaviour in an enterprise?

    A. Publishing Operating Principles

    B. Communicating Skill categories

    C. Appointing Business champions

    D. Publishing Delegation of Authority procedures

32. Which aspect relates to the COBIT 5 key principle 'Applying a Single Integrated Framework'?

    A. Aligns with the latest views on Governance

    B. Provides a simple architecture

    C. Translates Stakeholder needs into strategy

    D. Defines the relationship between Governance and Management

33. Who is an internal stakeholder?

    A. A customer

    B. A business partner

    C. A regulator

    D. A business executive

34. When designing an implementation plan for the governance and management of IT, what is an environmental factor that should be taken into consideration?

    A. Complex IT operating Models

    B. Hidden and rogue IT spending

    C. Applicable laws and regulations

    D. External audit or consultant assessments

35. Which attribute does NOT apply to a Process Activity?

    A. Considers the input and outputs of the process

    B. Supports establishment of clear roles and responsibilities

    C. Describes a set of implementation steps to achieve a management practice

    D. Provides statements of actions to deliver benefits

36. Identify the missing word in the following sentence.

    The responsibilities of Management include planning and monitoring activities in alignment with the direction set by the governance body to achieve the [?] objectives.

    A. enabler

    B. stakeholder

    C. IT-related

    D. enterprise

37. What is the term used to describe the values by which the enterprise wants to operate?

    A. Intrinsic quality

    B. Organisational ethics

    C. Individual ethics

    D. Good practices

38. Which business tool is used to justify business investments?

    A. Business objectives

    B. Business case

    C. Business policies

    D. Process Capability model

39. Which statement is NOT a reason why COBIT 5 is an integrated framework?

    A. It is complete in enterprise coverage

    B. Provides a simple architecture

    C. Has to be used with other standards

    D. Operates with previous ISACA frameworks

40. Identify the missing words in the following sentence.

    Business processes transform knowledge in order to create [?] for an enterprise.

    A. IT Processes

    B. information

    C. data

    D. value

41. Which dimension(s) deals specifically with the Process Reference Model?

    A. The Capability Dimension

    B. The Process Dimension

    C. The Enabler Dimension

    D. Both the Process and Capability Dimensions

42. Which item is a Service capability to deliver internal and external services?

    A. Frameworks

    B. Information

    C. Intrinsic Goal

    D. Contextual Goal

43. What does a 'Lead Indicator' measure?

    A. If enabler goals are achieved

    B. If stakeholder needs are addressed

    C. If governance is managed

    D. If good practices are applied

44. What is the specific information criteria called if it meets only the need of the information consumer?

    A. Compliant

    B. Believability

    C. Ease of operation

    D. Effective

45. What component of the Implementation Life Cycle addresses behavioural and cultural aspects of the implementation?

    A. Management of the programme

    B. Enablement of Change

    C. Core continual improvement life cycle

    D. Defining the road map

46. Which option is NOT a component of phase 3 in the Implementation Life Cycle?

    A. Identify role players

    B. Define Target state

    C. Communicate the Outcome

    D. Define the road map

47. What component of the Implementation Life Cycle addresses the question 'how do we get there'?

    A. Define problems and opportunities

    B. Enable new approaches

    C. Monitor and evaluate

    D. Implement improvements

48. In the PRM, what element provides an overview of what the process does?

    A. A process purpose

    B. A process identification

    C. A process description

    D. A process goal and metric

49. In a RACI chart, how is the role of someone who is Responsible for a task described?

    A. Someone who provides input to the task

    B. Someone who gets the task done

    C. Someone who is answerable for the success of the task

    D. Someone who is receiving information on a task

50. Which option is NOT a benefit to the enterprise of using the COBIT 5 framework?

    A. COBIT 5 is first and foremost a 'business framework'

    B. COBIT 5 is a framework to be used mainly for IT Service management

    C. COBIT 5 enables IT to be managed in a holistic manner

    D. COBIT 5 encourages a common language throughout the enterprise

Appendix M - Answerkey for COBIT 5 Sample Paper

Question #	Correct answer	Page	Question #	Correct answer	Page
1	A	13-14	26	B	15
2	A	16	27	A	27
3	C	32-33	28	B	4-5
4	C	15	29	A	15
5	A	14	30	C	28
6	D	27	31	C	20
7	D	6	32	B	7
8	A	19	33	D	16
9	C	15	34	C	31
10	D	46	35	D	17
11	C	18-22	36	D	9
12	D	45	37	B	20
13	C	16	38	B	34
14	C	41	39	C	7
15	D	4	40	D	21
16	B	18	41	B	41-42
17	D	7, 9	42	B	22
18	B	31-32	43	D	14
19	B	25-26	44	D	43
20	A	25	45	B	32
21	C	45	46	A	32
22	C	28	47	D	32-33
23	A	5	48	C	25
24	D	16	49	B	26
25	D	3	50	B	1, 8

NOTE: This publication is directed to readers that are interested in understanding the key terms, principles and facts of COBIT 5 at a foundation level and to those learners interested in achieving the COBIT 5 Foundation certification. To ease self-study, the publication has images and tables that contains important and relevant information so please do not pass them over when preparing for the real exam. *A picture says more than many words and 90% of the information that the brain process is visual.*

Index

5 principles of cobit 3
access & security 16
architecture principles 25
attribute rating 30, 33
contextual goal 18
contextual quality 16
enabler 10
enabler dimension 15
goals cascade 6
governance 3, 11
governance enablers 8
governance processes 12
governance scope 8
implementation lifecycle 34
information model 23
intrinsic goal 18
intrinsic quality 16
IT Governance 3
lag indicators 16
lead indicators 16
management processes 12
outcome 18
pain point 33, 36
process 18
process assessment model 29
process attribute 30, 33, 36
process capability levels 30
process capability model 29
process goal 18
process practices 27
process reference model 27
roles, activities and relationships 8
trigger event 33
value creation 5, 6, 9, 15

CPSIA information can be obtained at www.ICGtesting.com
Printed in the USA
LVIW01n1146020617
536734LV00011B/106